A SURVEY OF THE
OLD TESTAMENT
WORKBOOK

A SURVEY OF THE
OLD TESTAMENT
WORKBOOK

ANDREW E.   JOHN H.
HILL & WALTON
WITH JENNIFER M. HALE

ZONDERVAN
ACADEMIC

ZONDERVAN ACADEMIC

A Survey of the Old Testament Workbook
Copyright © 2018 by Andrew E. Hill and John H. Walton

This title is also available as a Zondervan ebook.

Requests for information should be addressed to:
Zondervan, *3900 Sparks Dr. SE, Grand Rapids, Michigan 49546*

978-0-310-55696-1

Cover design: Tammy Johnson
Cover photo: Todd Bolen/www.BiblePlaces.com
Interior design: Kait Lamphere

Printed in the United States of America

23 24 25 26 27 28 29 30 31 32 33 34 35 36 37 /PHP/ 18 17 16 15 14 13 12 11 10 9 8 7 6 5 4 3 2

TABLE OF CONTENTS

PART I: INTRODUCTION

PART II: THE PENTATEUCH

PART III: THE HISTORICAL BOOKS

PART IV: THE POETIC BOOKS

PART V: THE PROPHETS

Part I

INTRODUCTION

1

APPROACHING THE OLD TESTAMENT

NAME   DATE

A. OVERVIEW QUESTIONS

1. What does it mean to allow the Bible "to speak from its own vantage point"? How does one apply this methodology?

2. What is the objective of the Old Testament? Explain.

3. What is the primary interest of the history in the Old Testament?

4. What is God's plan?

5. Number the stages of God's presence in order from earliest to latest.

    _____Tabernacle/temple
    _____Incarnation
    _____New Creation
    _____Covenant
    _____Eden
    _____Pentecost
    _____Exodus

6. Define "covenant." How does God use the covenant in his self-revelation?

7. True/False: The written Word has authority, but the reader's response does not. (circle your answer)

8. What is NOT an implication of the authority of the Old Testament? (circle your answer)

    a. We need to respond to God's self-revelation.

    b. We need to try to find the message the author intended to communicate.

    c. We need to accept what the Old Testament says as truth.

    d. We need to search for the hidden meaning and mystical symbolism of each passage.

    e. all of the above

9. Define "storyline." Define "plotline." What is the difference?

10. True/False: Proper interpretation requires readers to throw away all presuppositions. (circle your answer)

11. Why is it important to identify the genre of the part of the Bible you are trying to interpret?

12. Since the Old Testament is God's self-revelation, what can you expect to learn in most instances?

B. THINK ABOUT IT

1. Go back and read one of your favorite Old Testament stories or passages. As best you can, identify the genre of the passage. What do you think the original author intended as the message? What do you learn about God from this passage? Has your interpretation of this passage changed at all after reading this chapter?

2. In your own words, describe what is meant by the phrase "inspiration of Scripture." What about the phrase "authority of Scripture"? How does the methodology presented in this chapter honor the inspiration and authority of the Old Testament?

2

GEOGRAPHY OF THE
OLD TESTAMENT

NAME ▨▨▨▨▨▨▨▨▨▨▨▨▨▨▨▨▨▨▨▨▨▨▨   DATE ▨▨▨▨▨▨▨▨▨▨

A. OVERVIEW QUESTIONS

1. Which regions do the Old Testament narratives encompass?

2. Four-fifths of Old Testament history take place where?

3. What area was considered the Fertile Crescent?

4. What does the name Mesopotamia mean?

5. Define the following key terms.

    a. wadi:

    b. steppe:

    c. alluvial:

    d. Levant:

    e. Apis:

    f. Baal:

6. Where was the Hittite Empire located during the second millennium BC?

7. Where was the land of covenant-promise for the Hebrews located?

8. Name the two regions into which ancient Egypt was divided. Which was located in the north and which in the south?

9. How is Egyptian influence seen in the language and literature of the Old Testament?

10. What were the lineages of the Moabites and Ammonites?

11. What was the Edomites' lineage? Where did they live?

12. Where did the Philistines settle?

13. What are the four basic geographical regions into which Palestine can easily be divided?

14. Where was the King's Highway located?

15. Why was the plateau area of the Transjordan region often the site of military conflict?

16. What were the names of the two international highways that linked Mesopotamia and Egypt via Palestine?

17. What was significant about the length of Israel's exile from the land?

18. Briefly outline the effects of the development of a merchant class in Israel.

B. GEOGRAPHY PROJECT

Fill out the following three maps according to the information in chapter 2, using outside resources if necessary.

Countries and Geographical Features
Countries

Number the countries according to the map on the next page.

_____Ammon

_____Aram (Syria)

_____Assyria

_____Babylonia

_____Edom

_____Egypt

_____Hittite Anatolia

_____Israel

_____Mitanni

_____Moab

_____Persia

_____Phoenicia

_____Sumer

Geographical Features

Letter the geographical features according to the map on the next page.

_____Black Sea

_____Caspian Sea

_____Dead Sea

_____Euphrates River

_____Gulf of Aqaba

_____Jordan River

_____Mediterranean Sea

_____Nile River

_____Persian Gulf

_____Red Sea

_____Sea of Galilee

_____Tigris River

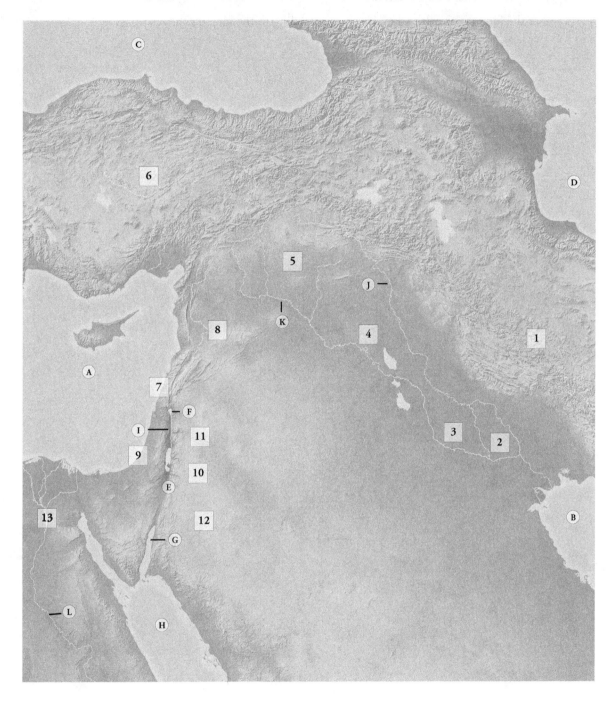

Foreign Capitals and Major Cities

Number the foreign capitals and major cities according to the map on the next page.

_____Babylon

_____Carchemish

_____Damascus

_____Emar

_____Hamath

_____Haran

_____Hattusha

_____Mari

_____Memphis

_____Nineveh

_____Nuzi

_____Sidon

_____Susa

_____Tyre

_____Ugarit

_____Ur

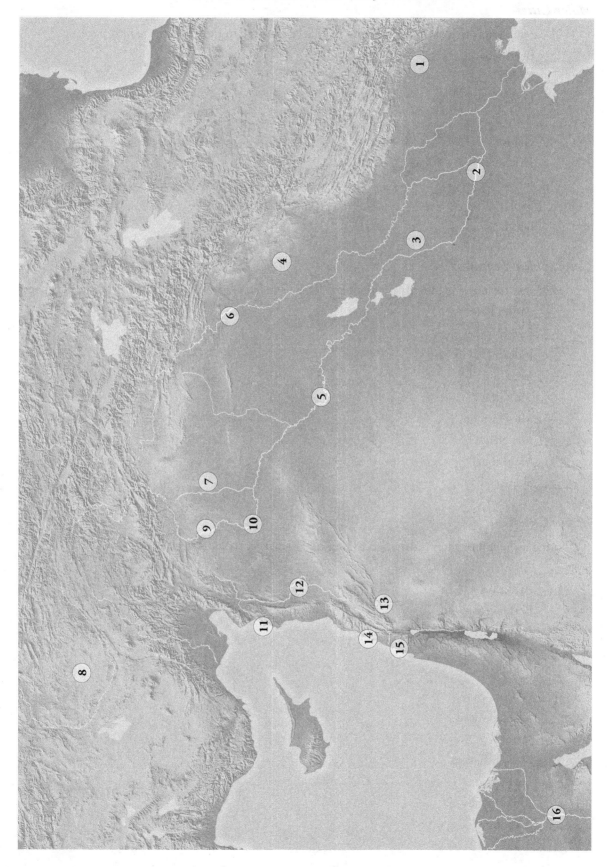

Major Cities and Geographical Features in Israel
Major Cities

Use capital letters to identify major cities in Israel according to the map on the next page.

_____Beersheba

_____Bethel

_____Dan

_____Hazor

_____Hebron

_____Jericho

_____Jerusalem

_____Samaria

_____Shechem

Geographical Features

Use lowercase letters to identify geographical features in Israel according to the map on the next page.

_____Arnon River

_____Jezreel Valley

_____Judean Hill Country

_____Mt. Carmel

_____Mt. Gilboa

_____Mt. Hermon

_____Mt. Nebo

_____Mt. Tabor

_____Shephelah

Minor Cities

Number the minor cities in Israel according to the map on the next page.

_____Ai

_____Ashkelon

_____Bethlehem

_____Bethshean

_____Gaza

_____Gibeah

_____Gibeon

_____Jabesh-Gilead

_____Jezreel

_____Kadesh Barnea

_____Lachish

_____Mahanaim

_____Megiddo

_____Shiloh

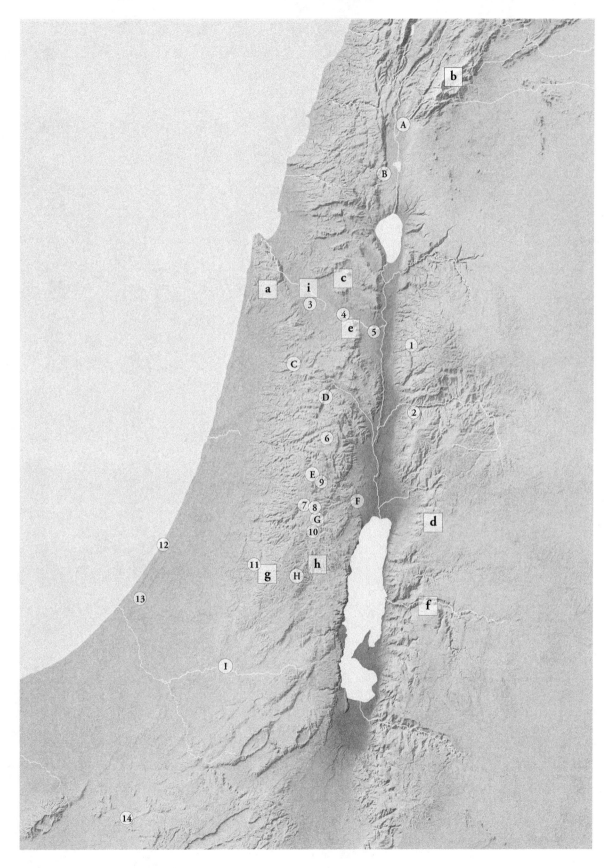

Part II

THE PENTATEUCH

3

INTRODUCTION TO
THE PENTATEUCH

NAME ████████████████████████████████ DATE ████████████████

A. OVERVIEW QUESTIONS

1. What books make up the Pentateuch? What does the word *Pentateuch* mean? What is the term the Hebrew-speaking Jewish community used for this group of books?

2. Into how many divisions is the Pentateuch divided, according to D. J. A. Clines? How were these divisions defined?

3. The prose of the Pentateuch is: (circle your answer and defend)

   a. a record of chronologically ordered events

   b. pointed religious propaganda

   c. saga

   d. folklore

   e. legend

   f. something else entirely or some mix of the above elements

4. What are the two types of genre in the Pentateuch where prophetic revelation takes place?

5. What was the purpose of Old Testament legislation?

6. List and define the subcategories of Old Testament law. (There are five.)

7. Define the following key terms.

   a. suzerain:

   b. vassal:

   c. date formula:

   d. literary criticism:

   e. Dominion Theology:

   f. covenant theology:

   g. tradition history:

8. What are the three schools of thought pertaining to the historicity of the Pentateuch? Briefly describe the stance of each.

B. BACKGROUND STUDY

1. What are the names of some of the ancient law collections that may have influenced the form and function of Hebrew law?

2. What is meant by the term "covenant law," and which ancient civilization's covenants are most similar to the Old Testament law material?

3. Name and define the three subheadings of ancient Near Eastern law.

4. Genesis 12–Deuteronomy 34 likely occurred during which of the ancient Near Eastern ages? What are some possible dates for the patriarchal period?

5. What are the options for the date of the exodus? Briefly describe the pros/cons for each position.

C. THINK ABOUT IT

1. What are the key similarities and differences between the old and new covenants? How do you reconcile the so-called harsh nature of the old covenant with the grace-filled nature of the new? Is this even a fair contrast?

2. Read 2 Timothy 3:16. How does this verse apply to Old Testament law?

D. READING CHALLENGE

1. Read Exodus 15 and Genesis 49. How can you tell these are poetic passages? How are they different from each other?

2. Read Leviticus 11, Deuteronomy 14, Mark 7:14–23, and Acts 10:9–23. How should Christians explain the relationship between these passages?

RESEARCH PROJECT 1
Chapters 3–9

Pick an ancient Near Eastern region (Palestine, Mesopotamia, or Egypt) and research some of the major events or cultural standards that may have been present during the lifetimes of either Abraham or Moses. (For useful resources, see the "For Further Reading" section on pp. 200–201 of your textbook.) Prepare a one to two-page report according to your professor's specifications.

1. List at least two major events or interesting sociological/economical structures that may have had an impact on Abraham or Moses.
2. Can you see evidence of this event or social structure in the Pentateuch? Explain.
3. Describe how this research does or does not affect your understanding of the biblical material.

RESEARCH PROJECT 2
The Exodus

Research the theories regarding an early or late date for the exodus. (For some sample resources, see "For Further Reading" on pp. 121–23.) Prepare a three- to five-page report or ten-minute presentation according to your professor's specifications. Be sure to include the following:

1. Briefly describe both positions and pick the position you prefer (or if you cannot decide, state why).
2. Discuss the genre of the exodus story and how this has affected your answer to #1.
3. Explain how, if at all, this research has affected your view of the historicity of the Pentateuch.

4

GENESIS

NAME ▓▓▓▓▓▓▓▓▓▓▓▓▓▓▓▓▓▓▓▓▓▓▓▓▓▓   DATE ▓▓▓▓▓▓▓▓▓▓▓▓▓▓

A. Overview Questions

1. The book of Genesis is primarily composed of: (circle your answer)

   a. science

   b. biographies

   c. history

   d. theology

   e. all of the above

   f. b, c, and d

2. Who was the author of Genesis?

3. Describe the *toledoth* formula. List two or three references where this formula appears.

4. Define the following key terms.

   a. comparative studies:

   b. "Founder's Stories":

c. sin:

d. covenant:

e. primeval history:

f. monotheism:

g. soteriology:

5. Could God's covenant with Abraham be canceled? Why or why not?

6. Was Abraham a monotheist? How does this affect your view of the narrative?

7. What is/are the message(s) of Genesis?

B. BACKGROUND STUDY

1. Name an ancient Near Eastern source that contains parallels to Genesis and describe the parallels. Describe the differences.

2. Does the existence of ancient Near Eastern parallel texts affect the Christian's view of inspiration and/or the historicity of Genesis? Why or why not?

3. The patriarchal narratives should be viewed against which archaeological periods?

4. How did the ancient peoples think about existence?

C. KEY PEOPLE

Add the following people to the chart in the back of the book (Appendix A).

  a. Abraham

  b. Adam

  c. Cain, Abel, and Seth

  d. Esau

  e. Eve

  f. Isaac

  g. Ishmael

  h. Jacob

  i. Joseph

  j. Laban

  k. Leah

  l. Levi

  m. Lot

  n. Manasseh (There are two major people with this name in the Old Testament. Find the one in Genesis.)

  o. Melchizedek

p. Noah

q. Potiphar

r. Rachel

s. Rebekah

t. Sarah

u. Shem, Ham, and Japheth

D. THINK ABOUT IT

1. Given the genre of Genesis and ancient Near Eastern background, what do *you* think is the purpose of Genesis 1? Give evidence for your answer.

2. Give two examples from the book of Genesis where we see both God's justice and his mercy.

3. How would you explain the flood or the tower of Babel saga to a friend who doesn't know the Bible very well?

4. Put yourself in the shoes of an ancient Israelite. Why is Joseph's story important? What does it tell you about God and his plan?

5. Why is it important to keep background material in mind while making modern-day theological applications? Give an example where this information has changed/enhanced your view of a passage in Genesis.

E. Reading Challenge

Pick one of the following passages below and describe (1) the major events and people; (2) the significance for the entire Old Testament; (3) the purpose; (4) the theological themes; and (5) the significance for today. (There may be more than one element per category for the section you choose.)

1. Genesis 1:1–3:24
2. Genesis 6:1–9:17
3. Genesis 15:1–17:27
4. Genesis 27:1–29:30
5. Genesis 37; 39:1–41:57

5

EXODUS

NAME _____   DATE _____

A. OVERVIEW QUESTIONS

1. List the five major themes of Exodus and give a corresponding Scripture reference for each theme.

2. What is the "redemptive event" of the Old Testament? Why do you think this event has such a status?

3. What is the conclusion most adherents of the Documentary Hypothesis hold regarding the authorship of Exodus?

4. Which four sections of the book confirm Mosaic authorship? Which sections suggest a later compiler?

5. What is the basic theological purpose of the book of Exodus? What is the basic didactic purpose?

6. Define the following key terms.

    a. divine oracle formula:

    b. Decalogue:

    c. miracle:

7. Identify the three narrative sections of the book of Exodus.

8. What is the Passover? What does it celebrate?

9. What does "I AM" connote? Why would its revelation to the people of Israel be significant?

10. Is it significant that Yahweh gives the Ten Commandments from heaven? Why do you think the commandments are given with the most severe negation possible in the Hebrew language?

B. BACKGROUND STUDY

1. Briefly describe the early date theory. What are its pros and cons?

2. Briefly describe the late date theory. What are its pros and cons?

3. List the three route theories associated with the exodus.

4. Pick one of the route theories you listed for number 3 and draw that route on the map below.

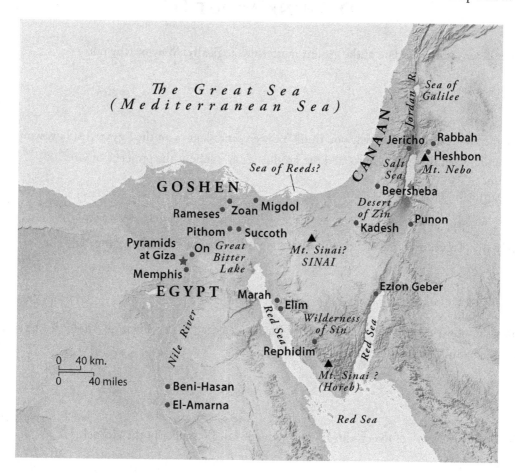

5. The Hebrew covenant with Yahweh parallels which type of Hittite treaty? Why is this significant?

6. How would blotting out the sun in Egypt while it remained daylight in Goshen be a significant message to the Egyptians?

C. KEY PEOPLE

Add the following people to the chart in the back of the book (Appendix A).

a. Aaron

b. Moses

c. Miriam

D. THINK ABOUT IT

1. Does determining the date of the exodus matter theologically? Why or why not?

2. If someone were to ask you why you think Yahweh sent plagues on the Egyptians, how would you respond? What do these plagues and the exodus teach us about the presence of God?

3. Were the plagues supernatural events or the intensification of natural phenomena? Why?

4. How should we explain the "hardening" of Pharaoh's heart? Is this situation similar to the sin of blasphemy in Mark 3:28–30? Explain your answer.

5. What does the story of the exodus reveal about the Lord's Supper in the Gospels?

6. How was the Decalogue an extension of the grace of God?

E. READING CHALLENGE

Read Exodus 3–4. Make a list of everything you learn about God in these two chapters. Why is God's revelation of himself in these two chapters important?

6

LEVITICUS

NAME ▓▓▓▓▓▓▓▓▓▓▓▓▓▓▓▓▓▓▓▓▓▓▓▓▓▓▓▓▓▓▓   DATE ▓▓▓▓▓▓▓▓▓▓▓▓▓▓▓▓▓▓▓▓▓

A. OVERVIEW QUESTIONS

1. Why were all the purity laws and legislation in Leviticus necessary?

2. To whom has the authorship of Leviticus been attributed traditionally? Why?

3. To what source do biblical scholars who hold to the Documentary Hypothesis attribute Leviticus? Why?

4. List some of the reasons why some biblical scholars argue for the authenticity and antiquity of Leviticus.

5. What is an indication that the books of Leviticus and Exodus are interrelated?

6. What is meant by the term "holiness" in Leviticus?

7. What are the two categories of sacrifices as described in Leviticus?

8. True/False: The animal sacrifices in Leviticus were intended to save the people from their sins. (circle your answer)

9. True/False: The animal sacrifices were intended to preserve a healthy relationship between God and the people. (circle your answer)

10. What is the importance of Sabbath rest and the sabbatical year within the book of Leviticus? Why do you think so much time is dedicated to laws concerning rest and restoration?

B. BACKGROUND STUDY

1. List three ways in which the Hebrew cultic religion differed from other ancient Near Eastern religions. List references to support your findings.

2. List two ways in which the Hebrew cultic religion was similar to other ancient Near Eastern religions.

C. THINK ABOUT IT

1. Read Leviticus 26–27. What appears to be the purpose of Leviticus? Use your own words.

2. Read John 1:29–34. What significance is there to the title the "Lamb of God"?

3. Why do you think there were not sacrifices outlined in Leviticus for premeditated or malicious covenant transgression?

4. Why do you think the book of Leviticus is preserved in the canon?

D. Reading Challenge

Pick two of the following passages below and describe (1) the reason for the use of each offering and (2) the animal or substance sacrificed. (3) Provide a chronological outline of the process for offering the sacrifices and (4) explain how the two offerings differ.

1. Burnt offering (Lev 1)
2. Meal offering (Lev 2)
3. Peace offering (Lev 3, 22)
4. Sin offering (Lev 4)
5. Guilt offering (Lev 5:1–67)

7

NUMBERS

NAME ░░░░░░░░░░░░░░░░░░░░░░░░░░░░░░░░   DATE ░░░░░░░░░░░░░░░░░░░░

A. OVERVIEW QUESTIONS

1. What is the Hebrew title of the book, and where did it come from?

2. Describe two of the possible authorship theories for the book of Numbers. Which seems more likely? Support your answer.

3. Match the events in the book of Numbers with the correct time frame.

    _____20 days
    _____38 years
    _____6 months

    a. from Kadesh to the plains of Moab

    b. at Mount Sinai

    c. of wilderness wandering

4. What is the twofold message of Numbers?

5. Why does the book appear disjointed? What does this imply about its composition?

6. Describe the theories that attempt to explain the large census numbers, listing any pros and cons.

7. Define the following key terms.

    a. supracultural:

    b. Documentary Hypothesis:

    c. seer:

B. BACKGROUND STUDY

1. Can we date the wanderings in Numbers precisely? Why or why not?

2. Trace the possible wilderness wanderings of the Israelites during the book of Numbers on the next page. Mark "#" where the census may have taken place. Circle Kadesh, Moab, and the Plains of Moab. Briefly describe the major events that occurred in these circled locations.

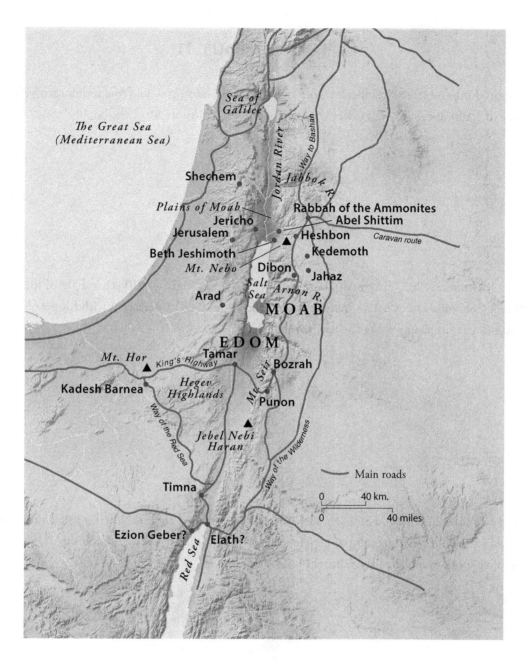

C. KEY PEOPLE

Add the following people to the chart in the back of the book (Appendix A).

a. Balaam

b. Balak

D. Think about It

1. Do you think the census numbers in Numbers are literal, or do you hold to another theory? Why? How (if at all) does your view affect your perception of the historicity of the book?

2. Read 1 Chronicles 29:17, Jeremiah 11:20, Psalm 139:23, and Isaiah 48:10–11 in light of the theology of Numbers. What do these verses tell you about God's interaction with his people? Does God still test his people under the new covenant?

3. Read Numbers 27:1–11 and 36:1–13. Here God has overturned ancient Near Eastern culture, but nowadays the line between cultural preference and theological sin is sometimes blurry. How does the Bible speak to modern-day culture? Or does it?

4. In Numbers 23–24 God talks to Balaam, a pagan diviner. Why do you think God found it necessary to speak to Balaam? Why were his words of cursing or blessing important?

E. READING CHALLENGE

Find one passage each within the book of Numbers that are examples of the following theological themes.

1. The holiness of God:
2. The sinfulness of humanity:
3. The necessity of obedience to Yahweh:
4. The tragedy of disobedience to Yahweh:
5. Yahweh's faithfulness to his covenant:

8

DEUTERONOMY

NAME ▨▨▨▨▨▨▨▨▨▨▨▨▨▨▨▨▨▨   DATE ▨▨▨▨▨▨▨▨▨▨

A. OVERVIEW QUESTIONS

1. What does the book of Deuteronomy summarize?

2. What are the two popular critical theories for which Deuteronomy has served as the basis?

3. What is the *Shema* and where is it found?

4. What are the four topical issues that the grouping of the material in Deuteronomy suggests? How are these topics addressed in commandments 1–4 versus 5–10?

5. How are chapters 6–11 different from chapters 12–26?

6. Explain what is meant by the following statement: "The second commandment is seen to go far beyond a prohibition against the use of idols" (p. 170).

7. Define the following key terms.

   a. divination:

8. Was the purpose of Deuteronomy to present a list of inflexible rules? Why or why not?

B. Background Study

1. Briefly describe the reasons for and against Mosaic authorship of Deuteronomy. Based on the evidence, what do you conclude?

2. What provides evidence for the unity of the book?

3. What type of treaty does the book of Deuteronomy most closely emulate?

4. What are the six elements of a standard treaty? List the parts of Deuteronomy that correspond to these elements. Where does Deuteronomy differ from the ancient form?

5. What is the difference between the laws in the Bible and the laws of the ancient Near East?

6. Why was centralization of the temple so important for Israel?

C. Think about It

1. How do the dietary commands of Deuteronomy relate to the third commandment? These commands are often described as "legalistic." How would you describe their purpose to a friend struggling with this issue?

2. Observing the Sabbath is one of the Ten Commandments, but it is most often not observed. Do you keep the Sabbath? Why or why not?

3. Reflect on this statement: "For [the ancient Israelite] there was hardly any greater display of God's grace than that demonstrated in his giving of the law" (p. 175). What is meant by this statement? Do you think it's true? How, if at all, does this change your view of the Old Testament?

D. READING CHALLENGE

1. Read Deuteronomy 6–11. Write down at least three examples from these chapters of how the Israelites were supposed to obey the first commandment. What did loving and honoring the Lord look like to the ancient Israelites? How do you think it should look for modern-day believers?

2. Now read Deuteronomy 16:18–18:22. How did honoring human authority look to ancient Israelites? How do you think it should look for modern-day believers?

9

HISTORICAL OVERVIEW OF OLD TESTAMENT TIMES

NAME _____   DATE _____

A. OVERVIEW QUESTIONS

1. What document contains the "fixed point" from which the chronology of the Old Testament and the ancient Near East can be determined? What specific event in this document provides the "fixed point"?

2. Which ancient country is the foundation for the chronology of the ancient Near East?

3. With whom/what event is the earliest synchronism of the Old Testament with the records of the ancient Near East?

4. Why does chronology remain controversial concerning the patriarchs and the period of the judges?

5. Why was Cyrus considered a deliverer rather than an oppressor?

CHRONOLOGY PROJECT

As you read through chapter 9, create four separate timelines. Use the time periods listed below and include the major events and kings listed for each respective timeline. Color code these events and kings according to the code listed for each timeline. If there is no designated color for the event, you may pick a color of your choice.

1. TIMELINE 1: 2900–1500 BC

Shade and Label

- Early Dynastic Period of Sumer
- Ur III Period
- Middle Bronze Age
- Old Kingdom of Egypt and the First Intermediate Period
- Hyksos Period

Include the Following Events

- Invention of writing
- Sargon I establishes the Semitic dynasty of Akkad
- Kingship of Ur-Nammu
- Kingship of Shulgi
- Hammurabi establishes the first dynasty of Babylon
- Hittite sack of Babylon
- Fall of Akkad
- Abraham's travels (estimate)
- Joseph in Egypt (estimate)
- The exodus (estimate)
- Israelites prosper and multiply in the delta region
- Akhenaten deserts Thebes
- Reign of Ramesses II (the Great)

Color Code			
Sumer	Red	Middle Bronze Age	Purple
Akkad	Yellow	Biblical figures/events	Blue
Ur	Green	Egypt	Orange
Babylon	Brown	Hyksos	Pink
Hittite	Black		

2. Timeline 2: 1500–950 BC

Shade and Label

- Late Bronze Age
- "Judges" period
- Iron Age I
- Iron Age II

Include the Following Events

- Emergence of the Hittites in Anatolia
- Battle at Qadesh
- Mitanni breaks apart
- Fall of the Hittite Empire
- Technological development of iron tools and weapons
- Destruction of the major port cities of Syria and of Megiddo and Ashkelon
- Reign of David
- Reign of Solomon
- Shishak sacks Jerusalem

Color Code			
Biblical figures/events	Blue	Hurrian	Yellow
Egypt	Orange	Iron Age I	Green
Late Bronze Age	Red	Iron Age II	Brown
Hittite	Black		

3. TIMELINE 3: 950–745 BC

Shade and Label

- Iron Age II

Include the Following Events

- Incursion of the Sea Peoples
- Reign of Hazael
- Campaigns of Ashurnasirpal II
- Battle at Qarqar
- Dynasty of Baasha
- House of Omri (include Ahab and Jezebel)
- Ministries of Elijah and Elisha
- "Purge" of Jehu
- Reign of Jeroboam II
- Reign of Azariah

Color Code			
Biblical figures/events	Blue	Arameans	Pink
Iron Age II	Brown	Assyrians	Red

4. TIMELINE 4: 745–450 BC

Shade and Label

- Reign of the Neo-Assyrian Empire
- Reign of the Neo-Babylonian Empire
- Reign of Nebuchadrezzar
- Reign of the Medo-Persian Empire
- Reign of Cyrus

Include the Following Events

- Reign of Tiglath-Pileser III
- Syro-Ephraimite war (battle with Rezin, Pekah, and Ahaz)
- Hoshea of Israel rebels against Assyria
- Three-year siege of Jerusalem by Shalmaneser V
- Fall of the Northern Kingdom of Israel
- Reign of Sargon II
- Reign of Sennacherib
- Hezekiah's deliverance
- Reign of Manasseh
- Reign of Esarhaddon
- Ashurbanipal captures Thebes
- Josiah's reforms
- Babylon declares independence from Assyria
- Fall of Nineveh
- Nebuchadrezzar storms Carchemish
- Death of Josiah
- Fall of Jerusalem
- Nehemiah rebuilds the wall

Color Code			
Biblical figures/events	Blue	Neo-Babylonian Empire	Red
Neo-Assyrian Empire	Orange	Medo-Persian Empire	Purple

Part III

THE HISTORICAL BOOKS

10

INTRODUCTION TO THE HISTORICAL BOOKS

NAME _____   DATE _____

A. OVERVIEW QUESTIONS

1. Which books are included in the English arrangement of the historical books?

2. Which books are considered "the Former Prophets"? What does this title imply about them?

3. Which books are considered "the Writings"?

4. Define the term "Deuteronomistic History." Who was the scholar who coined the term and which books are considered a part of it?

5. Who is the "Deuteronomist"?

6. What are some stylistic similarities within the books of the Deuteronomistic History? What are some dissimilarities?

7. Who is the main character of the historical books? (circle your answer)

    a. Joshua

    b. Samson

c. David

d. Elijah

e. Josiah

f. God

g. all of the above

8. Why were divination, omens, and incantations prohibited to the Israelites by law?

B. BACKGROUND STUDY

1. Explain the ancient Near Eastern concept of cause and effect and history. Why would this system result in the merging of history and theology?

2. Define "historiography." What type of historiography do we find in the ancient Near East? What about Israel?

C. THINK ABOUT IT

1. The books of Kings mention using sources. Does this affect your view of biblical inspiration? Why or why not?

2. Should we read these historical books like textbooks? Why or why not?

D. Reading Challenge

Read one of the following passages and discuss (1) why you think the story was included in biblical history; (2) who the hero of the story is; and (3) what the modern theological application of the story should be.

1. Judges 13–16
2. 1 Samuel 17–19
3. 1 Kings 17–18
4. 2 Kings 22–23:30

RESEARCH PROJECT 1
Chapters 10–19

Pick one of the following civilizations and research a religious cult that would have been popular during pre- or postexilic times.

1. Samaritan
2. Persian
3. Greek

Use secondary sources (like those listed in "For Further Reading" on pp. 213–14) to assist you as you:

a. Give a brief overview of the cult you studied.
b. Cite any references in the books of Kings, Chronicles, or Ezra–Nehemiah where practices from that religion may have been practiced by Israelites/Judahites or where it may have been reprimanded.
c. Describe why you think paganism and idolatry were so harshly punished in these historical books.

RESEARCH PROJECT 2
Chapters 10–19

Pick one of the following passages to study.

1. 2 Samuel 24:1; 1 Chronicles 21:1
2. 2 Samuel 23:8; 1 Chronicles 11:11
3. 2 Chronicles 33:18–20

Research these passages and the arguments that have been made for or against historical reliability. Include the following in your report.

a. A brief overview of the major arguments involved.
b. Your opinion regarding the arguments, along with your reasoning.
c. A theological reflection from your research.

❧ 11 ❧

JOSHUA

NAME ⟨blank⟩   DATE ⟨blank⟩

A. Overview Questions

1. Define the following key terms.

   a. hexateuch:

   b. Deuteronomistic school:

   c. etiological legend:

   d. Hyksos:

2. What is the purpose of the book of Joshua?

3. What are the four main sections of the book of Joshua? Include chapter delineations.

B. Background Study

1. What are some reasons for an early date for the book of Joshua's composition?

2. What is the date range within which the events of Joshua surely took place?

3. Name a few of the most prosperous seaports on the Syrian coast.

4. Why did city-state kings in Palestine and Syria write letters to the Egyptians? Why did diminished Egyptian control cause problems?

5. Who were the major players in the battle at Qadesh? What was the outcome of that battle?

6. Regardless of the date of the conquest, what role did Egyptian influence play in the conquest?

7. Label the tribal territories on the map below (Reuben, Simeon, Naphtali, Issachar, Asher, Dan, Zebulun, Gad, Benjamin, Judah, Manasseh, and Ephraim).

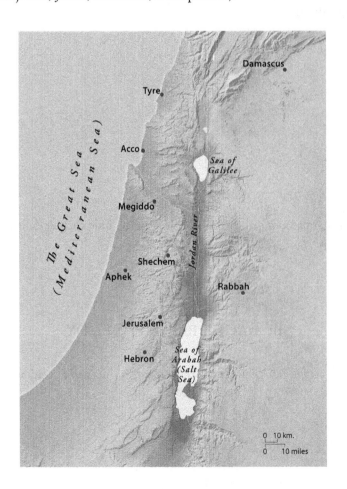

C. KEY PEOPLE

Add the following people to the chart in the back of the book (Appendix A).

    a. Joshua

    b. Caleb

    c. Achan

    d. Korah

    e. Rahab

D. THINK ABOUT IT

1. After considering the arguments for and against the historicity of the book of Joshua, do you think the book is a collection of etiological legends, or do you accept its historicity? Why have you chosen this position? How does your answer affect your theology?

2. The "ban" in Joshua is a difficult theological concept. How would you explain the reason for the "ban" of the peoples in the land to a friend? How do you reconcile this with your knowledge of God from other parts of the canon?

3. Read Joshua 7. In your own words, describe the concept of corporate solidarity. Compare and contrast ancient and modern conceptions of corporate and individual responsibility.

E. Reading Challenge

Pick one of the passages below and answer the following questions. (1) In your own words, how would you describe the message of your passage? (2) How does this message relate to the overall message of the book? (3) What major themes from the book do you see expounded in this passage? In what way are they expounded?

1. Joshua 2; 5:13–6:27
2. Joshua 9–10
3. Joshua 23–24

12

JUDGES

NAME   DATE

A. OVERVIEW QUESTIONS

1. Whom does Jewish tradition identify as the author of Judges? What is modern scholarship's consensus regarding the authorship of Judges?

2. What is the purpose of the book of Judges?

3. By what phrase is each cycle in chapters 3–16 introduced? What does this reveal theologically?

4. How is the mercy of God evident despite the Israelites' rebellion?

5. Briefly outline the judges cycles. What is significant about the Israelites' cry for help?

6. Why did the Israelites need a king, as inferred from Judges?

7. The tasks of the judges were primarily: (circle your answer)

    a. military in nature

    b. civil in nature

    c. spiritual in nature

    d. all of the above

    e. none of the above

8. True/False: The judges should be viewed as spiritual heroes who made ethical decisions. (circle your answer)

9. What elements determine whether a judge is a "major" or "minor" figure?

10. How is the empowerment of the spirit of the Lord different from the baptism of the Holy Spirit found in the New Testament?

11. Define the following key term.

    a. theocracy:

12. How were Israelite monotheism and Canaanite polytheism mutually exclusive?

B. BACKGROUND STUDY

1. Why is it likely that the judges period cannot be limited to Iron Age I?

2. How do scholars account for the number of years recorded in Judges?

3. Why did the author of Judges ignore the struggles of the major empires in his or her account?

4. What event provided for the growth of Philistine influence and the infiltration of the Aramaean tribes?

C. KEY PEOPLE

Add the following people to the chart in the back of the book (Appendix A).

a. Delilah

b. Ehud

c. Deborah

d. Barak

e. Samson

f. Othniel

g. Jephthah

D. THINK ABOUT IT

1. Read Judges 11. Did Jephthah do the right thing in keeping his vow? Why or why not? Why do you think this story is included in the narrator's theological-historical account?

2. Read Judges 16:23–31. Why do you think Samson was empowered by the Spirit in this situation? What does this demonstrate about God, the judges, and Israel during this time period?

E. Reading Challenge

Pick one of the passages below and answer the following questions. (1) What evidence do we have that Israel's morality was lacking? (2) What evidence is there that the judge in your story was ethical or unethical? (3) What do we learn about God's mercy and/or judgment in this story?

1. Judges 4–5
2. Judges 6–7

13

RUTH

NAME DATE

A. Overview Questions

1. The story of Ruth occurs during what time period?

2. Define the following key terms.

   a. Moabites:

   b. kinsman-redeemer:

   c. *ḥesed*:

   d. idyll:

3. What is the purpose of the narrative?

4. What was the intended purpose of levirate marriage?

5. To what does the term *ḥesed* refer? Where is it seen in Ruth?

B. BACKGROUND STUDY

1. To whom is authorship of Ruth attributed? During what time might it have been written?

2. Which judge may have been a contemporary of Ruth?

3. Who is the famous ancestor of the Moabites?

C. KEY PEOPLE

Add the following people to the chart in the back of the book (Appendix A):

a. Ruth

b. Boaz

c. Naomi

D. THINK ABOUT IT

1. Can ancient Near Eastern knowledge about the kinsman-redeemer and the nature of redemption as it applies to Old Testament law be applied to our understanding of the concept of redemption in the New Testament? If so, how?

E. READING CHALLENGE

Read the book of Ruth. How does this narrative differ from the accounts of Judges? What background does this knowledge provide for King David? What do you learn about God from this story? Why is it such an important story to have in the canon?

❧ 14 ❧

1–2 SAMUEL

NAME _____   DATE _____

A. Overview Questions

1. True/False: The books of 1 and 2 Samuel originally constituted a single book. (circle your answer)

2. How does the compiler of Samuel demonstrate that the Davidic covenant was established by God?

3. Do 1 and 2 Samuel portray a whitewashed image of David? Why or why not?

4. Why was the capture of the ark of the covenant a significant way to end the judges period? What did it symbolize?

5. Which chapters constitute the Shiloh traditions? What narratives are contained in these chapters?

6. Why did a human king not meet the people's expectations?

7. Why were the people being oppressed? Would a kingship help this problem?

8. Why does the compiler make so much of an effort to show the failures of Saul independently of David's influence?

9. Some allege that the treatment of Saul and David is nothing more than propaganda to legitimatize David's rise to the throne. Is this true? Why or why not?

10. Skim the Succession Narrative in 2 Samuel 10–20. What was the author's theological agenda for including this Succession Narrative?

11. What is the overall purpose of the books of Samuel?

12. How do we know that the presence of the ark in Jerusalem at the beginning of David's reign represented the Lord's approval?

13. What was wrong with the people's request for a king? (circle your answer)

    a. They should've been happy with a priest/judge like Samuel.

    b. Monarchies are bad.

    c. They expected that a human king could succeed where the Lord had failed.

    d. all of the above

    e. a and c

14. What is meant by the following statement: "The terminology used indicates that this [Davidic] covenant would better be described as open-ended rather than eternal" (p. 271)?

B. BACKGROUND STUDY

1. Why were the tribes forced to cooperate more during the time of Samuel than previously?

2. Why were idols prohibited in Israelite religious practice? How was the ark different from an idol?

C. Key People

Add the following people to the chart in the back of the book (Appendix A).

    a. Absalom

    b. Bathsheba

    c. Hiram

    d. Joab

    e. Nathan

    f. Eli

    g. Samuel

    h. Hannah

    i. Jonathan

    j. Saul

D. Think about It

1. Why is it significant that Jesus came from the line of David? What does this reveal about the term "Messiah," especially as it is used to describe Jesus?

2. Read 1 Samuel 28. What does this episode reveal about Saul?

3. David made many mistakes. What does his appointment by God (despite those errors) reveal about David? What does it reveal about God?

E. READING CHALLENGE

Read two of the passages below and answer the following questions. (1) What do you learn about God's grace, judgment, or covenants with Israel in these passages? (2) What relation do these passages have to other parts of the Old Testament? (3) What significance do these passages have for New Testament themes and theology?

1. 1 Samuel 1–3
2. 1 Samuel 16–17
3. 2 Samuel 11–12
4. 2 Samuel 16:15–18:18

❧ 15 ❧

1–2 KINGS

NAME ▒▒▒▒▒▒▒▒▒▒▒▒▒▒▒▒▒▒▒▒▒▒▒▒   DATE ▒▒▒▒▒▒▒▒▒▒

A. OVERVIEW QUESTIONS

1. Which books compose the "Former Prophets," and what types of literature are included therein?

2. Kings was originally part of a _____ volume collection. It was divided into _____ books in the _____ for convenience. (circle your answer)

    a. 2; 4; Vulgate

    b. 2; 4; Septuagint

    c. 4; 2; Vulgate

    d. 4; 2; Septuagint

3. Who is the author of Kings according to Jewish tradition? For those who disregard this theory but still hold to the traditional view, what characteristics can be attributed to the author?

4. Briefly describe the alternative view of authorship.

5. What are the sources referenced by the author of Kings? These resources were likely what type of document?

6. What is the purpose of the Kings narrative?

7. Briefly describe the characteristic formula that framed Judahite kingship.

8. To what did the author of Kings attribute the split of the Northern and Southern Kingdoms?

9. The development of Hebrew kingship prompted the emergence of what two parallel prophetic movements?

10. Define the following key terms.

   a. dynastic succession:

   b. Osiris:

11. What type of kingship was associated with the Southern Kingdom? Which type was associated with the Northern Kingdom?

B. BACKGROUND STUDY

1. What is a reasonable date for the completion of the Kings record?

2. For which time periods does the author of Kings record events?

3. What are two of the most outstanding archaeological finds related to the Kings account and why are they significant?

4. Under which king was Israel's "golden age"?

5. How did the actions of Elijah and Elisha refute Baal's power? Give references to support your answer.

6. Why would Jeroboam have brought the bull-god to Israel?

7. Where did Jeroboam erect shrines? Why?

C. KEY PEOPLE

Add the following people to the chart in the back of the book (Appendix A).

    a. Elijah

    b. Elisha

    c. Ahab

    d. Jezebel

    e. Jehu

    f. Jeroboam

    g. Queen of Sheba

D. THINK ABOUT IT

1. Read 1 Kings 11. What did Solomon do that was unwise? What do his actions and the Lord's response reveal about leadership, grace, and judgment?

2. Read 2 Kings 22–23. What does this episode reveal about the state of Judah? A few years after Josiah, Judah still ends up in exile. Why do you think this is? What does it reveal about God's covenant with David?

E. READING CHALLENGE

Read one of the passages below and answer the following questions. (1) What seems to be the purpose of your passage? What does it reveal about God? What does it reveal about the narrative of Israel? (2) Do you think the main characters in your story acted righteously? Why or why not? (3) Page 279 says, "The biblical narrative implicitly balances the notion of God's sovereignty and the reality of human freedom." Does this statement apply to your passage? If so, how? If not, does your passage emphasize one or the other?

1. 1 Kings 17–19
2. 2 Kings 4–7:2
3. 2 Kings 9–10

❧ 16 ❧

1–2 CHRONICLES

NAME   DATE

A. Overview Questions

1. What book does Chronicles follow in the Hebrew Bible, and what does this suggest?

2. From where is the Hebrew title ("the words of the days") of Chronicles taken? What is its Greek title? Where does the English title come from?

3. What is the likely identity of the compiler of Chronicles? Why do many scholars think this?

4. List the five categories of sources used by the Chronicler.

5. Define/identify the following key terms.

    a. Ahura Mazda:

    b. inspired exposition:

    c. colophon:

    d. new exodus:

    e. theocratic ideal:

    f. typology:

6. What is meant by the term "theology of hope" as it relates to the chronicler? Can you find an example of this hope in the books of Chronicles?

7. Describe the typological link between Joshua and Solomon.

B. BACKGROUND STUDY

1. The books of Chronicles ignore which part of Israelite history? Why do you suppose this is so?

2. What does the Chronicler leave out regarding the reigns of David and Solomon? Why do you think he or she does this?

3. List three of the major pagan religious threats to the Israelite and Judahite communities.

C. KEY PEOPLE

Add the following people to the chart in the back of the book (Appendix A).

   a. Josiah

   b. Solomon

   c. Jehoshaphat

   d. Joash

   e. Athaliah

   f. Manasseh (There are two major people in the Old Testament with this name. List the one in Chronicles.)

g. Shishak

h. Rehoboam

D. THINK ABOUT IT

1. Why did the Chronicler focus so much on the reigns of David and Solomon? Give at least two possible reasons.

2. Describe the theme of worship as is found in the books of Chronicles. Pick a passage where worship is present (see pp. 321–23) and discuss what modern-day application should be drawn from it.

3. How do you think the Chronicler understood divine retribution?

E. READING CHALLENGE

Pick one of the following rulers and read the passages in Chronicles that concern his or her story (you may use the outline on pp. 310–11 for a guide). Explain whether the ruler you chose was righteous or wicked or some combination of the two and give evidence for your answer. What does this ruler's story demonstrate about divine retribution?

1. Rehoboam
2. Jehoshaphat
3. Athaliah
4. Joash
5. Hezekiah
6. Manasseh
7. Josiah

❧ 17 ❧

EZRA–NEHEMIAH

NAME _____   DATE _____

A. OVERVIEW QUESTIONS

1. Ezra was a _____ and a _____. (fill in the blanks)

2. Nehemiah is well known for: (circle your answer)

    a. rebuilding the wall of Jerusalem

    b. being a prophet

    c. being a scribe

    d. a and b

    e. all of the above

3. Ezra and Nehemiah form a _____ book from the _____ volume of a work put together by the Chronicler. (circle your answer)

    a. two-part; second

    b. single; second

    c. two-part; first

    d. single; first

4. Why is it assumed that the postexilic Chronicler edited the book of Ezra–Nehemiah?

5. Outline and describe the likely sequence of compilation for Ezra–Nehemiah.

6. In what language(s) was Ezra written? Why?

7. The second temple was: (circle your answer)

    a. grander than Solomon's temple

    b. slightly less grand than Solomon's temple

    c. as big but less decorated than Solomon's temple

    d. could not even compare to Solomon's temple and caused weeping among the returned exiles

8. Define the following key terms.

    a. Hellenism:

    b. Apocrypha:

    c. postexilic:

B. BACKGROUND STUDY

1. The reforms of Ezra and Nehemiah were directed against which covenant violations? Why is this significant?

2. List the possible dates for Ezra's arrival in Jerusalem. Which one seems most likely? Why?

3. List the kings of Persia (along with possible dates for their reigns) from Xerxes to Artaxerxes II. Under which kings did Ezra and Nehemiah live?

4. How has the historical reliability of these books been confirmed?

5. Trace the evolution of the scribe from preexilic Israel to postexilic Judah.

C. KEY PEOPLE

Add the following people to the chart in the back of the book (Appendix A).

    a. Cyrus

    b. Ezra

    c. Nehemiah

    d. Zerubbabel

D. THINK ABOUT IT

1. How did Ezra–Nehemiah provide hope to the postexilic community?

2. What were the beneficial effects of Ezra's combined role as priest-scribe and his appeal to the Mosaic law? What were some eventual negative effects? Provide evidence using references from the New Testament.

E. READING CHALLENGE

Pick one chapter from Ezra–Nehemiah and address the following issues.

1. Note the historical context.
2. Determine whether the passage would have offered hope, conviction, or something else to the postexilic community.
3. Explain what you can learn about God from the chapter.

❧ 18 ❧

ESTHER

NAME ▨▨▨▨▨▨▨▨▨▨▨▨▨▨▨▨▨   DATE ▨▨▨▨▨▨▨▨▨

A. OVERVIEW QUESTIONS

1. What about the book has prompted debate about its status as Scripture?

2. Who is the author of Esther?

3. What about the book has prompted debate about its historicity? How do we reconcile this with biblical inspiration?

B. BACKGROUND STUDY

1. What is Purim? What does it commemorate?

2. When was the book of Esther likely penned? Why?

3. What is the genre of Esther?

4. Who is the primary source of Persian history for this time period?

C. Key People

Add the following people to the chart in the back of the book (Appendix A).

    a. Xerxes

    b. Haman

    c. Esther

    d. Mordecai

    e. Darius the Great

D. Think about It

1. God is not mentioned in the book of Esther, but where can his actions be seen? List at least two references from the book as support.

2. Find an example of literary irony in the book. Why is this irony significant?

3. God often brings deliverance to his people in miraculous and powerful ways (i.e., the exodus). Why do you think the deliverance is more understated (though not less miraculous) in the book of Esther?

E. Reading Challenge

Read the book of Esther, pick one of the following questions, and give a short answer.

1. Does the fact that Esther is a woman play into biblical theology? Does it play into the theology of the book?
2. Compare and contrast Haman and Mordecai. What are their similarities? Differences? Are their states at the end of the book anticipated or a surprise?
3. Analyze Esther's, Mordecai's, and Haman's actions. Who is the hero of the book? Explain.

❧ 19 ❧

ARCHAEOLOGY AND THE OLD TESTAMENT

NAME ░░░░░░░░░░░░░░░░░░░░░░░░░░░ DATE ░░░░░░░░░░░░

A. Overview Questions

1. What is the purpose of archaeology?

2. What are the most common objects found in ancient Near Eastern archaeology?

3. What types of finds are the greatest contributions to an archaeologist's task?

4. Which of the following contributions has archaeology made to biblical studies? (circle all that apply)

   a. The construction of a historical framework

   b. Suggestions as to why the people of antiquity acted the way they did

   c. The provisions of historical fact

   d. Linguistics

   e. Reconstruction of political situations

   f. Affirmation of the sovereign role of God

5. True/False: Archaeology can authenticate history, but it cannot authenticate theology. (circle your answer)

6. Identify three of the major ancient Near Eastern archives that have been found and describe their significance for biblical investigation.

7. What was significant about the discovery of the Dead Sea Scrolls?

8. Match the description below by placing the correct letter next to the inscription.

    _____The Mesha Inscription
    _____The Stele of Shalmaneser III
    _____Sennacherib's Prism
    _____The Cyrus Cylinder

    a. Contains the royal decree granting various peoples permission to return.

    b. Speaks of western campaigns against coalitions that include kings Ahab and Jehu.

    c. Reports how Moab had come under the domination of Israel during the reign of Omri but had regained its independence and recaptured some territory.

    d. Notes increased tribute from King Hezekiah of Judah.

9. Where have major cultic sanctuaries been discovered in Israel without a statue of a deity?

10. Should archaeological evidence be accepted as an authority over and above the biblical account? Why or why not?

RESEARCH PROJECT

Research one of the ways that archaeology has provided insight for biblical investigation (reference to Belshazzar, David, Ramesses II, Hittites, etc.). Use secondary sources (see "For Further Reading" on pp. 370–71) and prepare a short report of your findings. Answer the following.

1. What finds have helped to provide a historical background for biblical material? In what way have they succeeded?
2. Pick a biblical passage that relates to your topic. Discuss how the archaeological find has changed or not changed your understanding of the passage.

Part IV

THE POETIC BOOKS

❧ 20 ❧

HEBREW POETIC AND WISDOM LITERATURE

NAME _____   DATE _____

A. OVERVIEW QUESTIONS

1. What is the fundamental feature that distinguishes Hebrew poetry from prose?

2. What is a "prose particle," and what are the densities necessary to determine prose or poetry?

3. Define the following key terms.

   a. oracular prose:

   b. wisdom (Hebrew):

   c. theodicy:

   d. rhythm of sound:

   e. rhythm of thought:

   f. retribution principle:

4. Is it wise to use modern linguistic methodology to analyze biblical poetry? Why or why not?

5. How much of the Old Testament is poetry? Which books contain little or no poetry?

6. Which books are considered wisdom books? List a couple portions of prophetic literature where wisdom terminology is used.

7. What are the two distinctive features of Hebrew poetry?

8. List the three basic types of parallelism in Hebrew poetry.

9. Briefly outline the evolution of the types of Hebrew poetry.

10. What are the two genres of wisdom literature in the Old Testament?

11. Describe the four wisdom speech forms. Give an example from Scripture of each type.

12. Circle the characteristics that are representative of godly wisdom.

   a. purity

   b. peace

   c. love

   d. pride

   e. drive

   f. gentleness

g. submission

h. mercy

i. impartiality

j. cunning

k. sincerity

B. BACKGROUND STUDY

1. To when can the rudiments of Egyptian poetry be traced?

2. What are the similarities between the Aten Hymn and Psalm 104? (See Figure 20.1a on p. 378.)

3. Underline the similarities between Egyptian Love Song 31 and Song of Songs 4:1–7.

EGYPTIAN LOVE SONG 31

One, the lady love without a duplicate,
more perfect than the world,
see, she is like the star rising
at the start of an auspicious year.
She whose excellence shines, whose body
glistens,
glorious her eyes when she stares,
sweet her lips when she converses,
she says not a word too much.
High her neck and glistening her nipples,
of true lapis her hair,
her arms finer than gold,
Her buttocks droop when her waist is girt,
her legs reveal her perfection;
her steps are pleasing when she walks
the earth,
she takes my heart in her embrace.

When she comes forth, anyone can see
that there is none like that One.*

SONGS OF SONGS 4:1–7

How beautiful you are, my darling!
    Oh, how beautiful!
    Your eyes behind your veil are doves.
Your hair is like a flock of goats
    descending from the hills of Gilead.
Your teeth are like a flock of sheep just shorn,
    coming up from the washing.
Each has its twin;
    not one of them is alone.
Your lips are like a scarlet ribbon;
    your mouth is lovely.
Your temples behind your veil
    are like the halves of a pomegranate.
Your neck is like the tower of David,
    built with courses of stone;
on it hang a thousand shields,
    all of them shields of warriors.
Your breasts are like two fawns,
    like twin fawns of a gazelle
    that browse among the lilies.
Until the day breaks
    and the shadows flee,
I will go to the mountain of myrrh
    and to the hill of incense.
You are altogether beautiful, my darling;
there is no flaw in you.

4. Do the similarities between the Teachings of Amenemope and Proverbs present a theological problem? Why or why not?

---

* From W. K. Simpson, ed., *The Literature of Ancient Egypt*, rev. ed. (New Haven: Yale University Press, 1973), 315–16.

5. What do the similarities between Ugaritic and Hebrew poetry suggest about their linguistic heritages?

6. What are the general differences between Hebrew wisdom literature and that of their ancient Near Eastern neighbors?

C. Think about It

1. What is meant by the expression "the fear of the Lord," and why do you think this particular concept distinguished the ancient Israelites from their ancient Near Eastern counterparts?

2. Reflect on the following statement: "Ultimately wisdom results in the ability to steer through life in a way that wins favor and a good name in the sight of both humanity and God" (p. 390). What does it mean in your own words? Can you give an example where this principle has applied in your own life?

D. Reading Challenge

Pick a psalm to study. With the seven literary techniques commonly used by Hebrew poets in mind (pp. 384–87), point out the techniques used in your psalm. Write the lines and your analysis below.

RESEARCH PROJECT
Chapter 20

Pick Proverbs, Job, or Ecclesiastes to research. Read a large section of the work that you chose and prepare a report that includes the following information, using secondary resources as necessary. (For some suggested secondary sources, see "For Further Reading" on pp. 397–99.)

1. A summary of the work's major ideological premises.
2. A comparison of this work's theological ideals with those of other ancient Near Eastern wisdom literature.
3. Based on your research, how should the principles within this work be understood?
4. What theological applications can be applied to your life from this study?

21

JOB

NAME ░░░░░░░░░░░░░░░░░░░░░░░░░░░░░░░░░░░░░   DATE ░░░░░░░░░░░░░░░░░

A. Overview Questions

1. What is the genre of Job? Were the speeches transcribed exactly as they happened?

2. What was likely Job's ethnicity? (circle your answer)

   a. Chaldean

   b. Israelite

   c. Edomite

   d. Sabaean

3. What is the purpose of the book of Job?

4. Who/what is on trial in the book of Job? (circle your answer)

   a. Job

   b. God

   c. God's policies

   d. Job's righteousness

5. Define the following key term.

    a. retribution principle:

6. What role do Job's friends play within the story?

7. Which attributes of God are emphasized in the book of Job?

B. BACKGROUND STUDY

1. Should the speeches of Elihu be considered secondary additions? Why or why not?

2. Does the wisdom literature of the ancient Near East have comparable compositions? Describe how ancient Near Eastern wisdom literature is similar to or different than the book of Job using the excerpts from Figures 21.1 and 21.2 (pp. 406–7).

3. Why is "the satan" not called "Satan" in the textbook?

C. KEY PEOPLE

Add the following person to the chart in the back of the book (Appendix A).

    a. Job

D. THINK ABOUT IT

1. Think back to a time when you or someone you love went through a difficult circumstance. Did you or they respond with retribution principle theology?

2. What can you learn from the book of Job about asking the "why me?" question? What can you learn from Job about asking the "why did you do this, God?" question?

3. Reflect on the following statement, "Since there was only one sovereign God, suffering could not come from any other source" (p. 414). Do you believe God causes suffering? Why or why not? Use Scripture in your answer.

E. READING CHALLENGE

Read Job 38–42. In your own words, state what God is telling Job. Why does God answer Job in this way? What do we learn about God from this interchange?

❧ 22 ❧

PSALMS

NAME ▓▓▓▓▓▓▓▓▓▓▓▓▓▓▓▓▓▓▓▓   DATE ▓▓▓▓▓▓▓▓▓▓▓▓

A. OVERVIEW QUESTIONS

1. When did the final composition of the book of Psalms take place?

2. From where does our main source of information regarding authorship come?

3. List the five books of the book of Psalms.

4. Which psalms are likely an introduction to the whole book? Why would a cohesive introduction be important?

5. True/False: The book of Psalms was compiled with a particular theological agenda in mind. (circle your answer)

6. What are the three general categories of psalms?

7. Define the following key terms.

   a. descriptive praise:

   b. declarative praise:

   c. cantata:

8. How should one determine the author's purpose in writing a psalm?

9. Which psalms make up the "seam" psalms, and why are they important?

10. What is/are the message(s) of Psalms 1 and 2?

11. True/False: Psalms as a book confirms the retribution principle. (circle your answer)

12. True/False: The book of Psalms implies that there will be no exceptions to the retribution principle. (circle your answer)

13. How was God's favor or disfavor inferred in ancient Israelite society as it pertained to nature? Why do you think the Israelites thought this way?

B. Background Study

1. To which ancient culture do Israelite lament psalms bear the most resemblance?

2. What are the two types of praise in Israelite psalms? Which type does not appear in Mesopotamian literature? Why might this be significant?

3. What are the differences between Israelite and Mesopotamian lament psalms?

C. THINK ABOUT IT

1. Pick one of the following psalms. Is it a praise, lament, or wisdom psalm? Why is it important to note the type of psalm before interpreting it?

   a. Psalm 51

   b. Psalm 3

   c. Psalm 96

   d. Psalm 111

2. Find a psalm that seems to wrestle with the question, "If God is a just God, how can the righteous suffer or the wicked prosper?" How does the psalmist tackle the question? How should *we* approach the issue in light of the New Testament?

3. Reflect on the following statement: "Affirmation of God's attributes is the goal of our devotional reading" (see p. 434). Do you agree? Why or why not?

D. Reading Challenge

Read one of the collections of psalms below. (1) List the common themes you find in your collection of psalms. (2) Why do you think these psalms were placed together in the Psalter? (3) What message do they seem to present? (4) What do you learn about God from these psalms? (5) How should they be applied to your life?

1. Psalms 111–17
2. Psalms 120–27
3. Psalms 138–45

❧ 23 ❧

PROVERBS

NAME ████████████████████████   DATE ████████████

A. OVERVIEW QUESTIONS

1. The book of Proverbs is essentially a collection of what? (Give a more detailed answer than "proverbs.")

2. Which sections of Proverbs are considered the oldest material in the book? To when do they date? Who is the likely author?

3. When (most likely) was the final composition of the book of Proverbs? Provide evidence for your answer.

4. List the three major divisions of proverbial literature.

5. Define the following key term.

    a. corpus:

6. What is the "vertical" dimension of covenant relationship? What is the "horizontal" dimension?

7. What are other translations for the words rendered "prosperity" in Proverbs 21:21 (NIV)? Why might this be significant?

B. BACKGROUND STUDY

1. Who were Agur and Lemuel? Which Proverbs are ascribed to them?

2. What were the reciprocal benefits of the practice of wisdom for Hebrew kingship and Hebrew society?

3. How was Hebrew wisdom literature similar to that of the Egyptians and Mesopotamians?

C. THINK ABOUT IT

1. What does it mean to apply "the fear of the LORD" to daily life? Give an example that applies to modern living.

2. How does the "fear of the LORD" prevent "proverbial wisdom from degenerating into a rigid and mechanistic system of cause and effect relationships" (p. 447)?

3. Why do you think Proverbs spends so much time on the subject of human speech?

4. Why do you think Proverbs spends so much time on the subject of human sexuality? Pick a verse on this issue and determine if its wisdom still applies in modern culture. Support your answer.

D. READING CHALLENGE

Read one of the passages below and answer the following questions. (1) Where do you see "the fear of the LORD" exemplified in this passage? (2) What seems to be the overarching goal of the proverbs you read (long life, prosperity, etc.)? (3) Do these proverbs support or undermine (or both) the retribution principle? Explain your reasoning.

 a. Proverbs 2–3
 b. Proverbs 5–7
 c. Proverbs 8–9

24

ECCLESIASTES

NAME ⬚⬚⬚⬚⬚⬚⬚⬚⬚⬚⬚⬚⬚⬚⬚⬚⬚⬚⬚⬚⬚⬚⬚⬚⬚⬚ DATE ⬚⬚⬚⬚⬚⬚⬚⬚⬚

A. OVERVIEW QUESTIONS

1. Who is Qoheleth?

2. Who is the traditional author of Ecclesiastes? What is the evidence for and against this postulation?

3. Is it necessary to date the authorship of the book precisely? Why or why not?

4. What is the message of Ecclesiastes?

5. Define the following key term.

   a. colophon:

6. True/False: Qoheleth views the retribution principle as conveying something about God but does not view it as a guarantee for life. (circle your answer)

B. BACKGROUND STUDY

1. What is the Dialogue of Pessimism? How does it relate to studies on Ecclesiastes?

2. Read the excerpt from the Harper's Song in Figure 24.1 (p. 458) in the textbook. How is it similar to Ecclesiastes? How is it different?

C. THINK ABOUT IT

1. Does the New Testament bring light to the questions presented by Qoheleth? Support your answer.

2. Reflect on the following statement: "Though nothing can offer fulfillment, one need not adopt a pessimistic, cynical, or fatalistic view toward life" (p. 461). How is this possible? How, then, should believers orient their thinking?

3. Why do you think that Qoheleth makes no reference to the Law, the Prophets, or God's covenant?

4. Reflect on the following statement: "Enjoyment of life comes not in the quest for personal fulfillment, but in the recognition that everything comes from the hand of God" (p. 464). Describe a modern-day situation where this philosophy would be helpful.

5. How can the theology of Qoheleth be applied in your everyday life? Should it be applied? Why or why not?

D. READING CHALLENGE

Read the book of Ecclesiastes in one sitting. Do you think Qoheleth's ponderings are an example of incorrect thinking? Or do you think the book demonstrates orthodox thinking? Support your answer with at least two references from the book.

❧ 25 ❧

SONG OF SONGS

NAME _____   DATE _____

A. OVERVIEW QUESTIONS

1. Why is Song of Songs placed alongside wisdom literature in the Septuagint and most English versions?

2. Why was Song of Songs read during the Passover Feast in later Judaism?

3. According to traditional scholarship, when and by whom was Song of Songs written?

4. What are some other options for authorship and date of composition?

5. Define the following key terms.

   a. provenance:

   b. Megilloth:

   c. allegory:

6. Match the descriptions below with the following approaches to the interpretation of Song of Songs.

   _____Dramatic
   _____Typological
   _____Cultic
   _____Wedding cycle

_____Didactic

_____Allegorical

_____Literal

a. A collection of nuptial poems similar to the *wasf* of Arabic wedding ceremonies.

b. An ancient Hebrew play or dramatic script intended for royal entertainment.

c. A presentation of the purity and wonder of sexual love; instruction on the virtues of human affection and marriage.

d. A historical account that is read as God's covenant relationship to Israel or Christ's relationship to the church.

e. God's covenant relationship to Israel or God's relationship to the church *not* based on a historical account.

f. An adaptation of Mesopotamian fertility cult liturgy; cultic association was forgotten or consciously changed to make the book acceptable to Israelite faith.

g. A sensual expression of passion as two young lovers voice their desire for each other.

7. What is Bullock's suggestion for interpretation? What is the main alternative to his interpretation?

B. BACKGROUND STUDY

1. Read 1 Kings 4:20–28, 10:14–29, and 11:1–3. What do these passages reveal about Solomon? What do they reveal about the possible setting of Song of Songs?

2. Is Song of Songs similar to or different from other ancient love poetry of the second millennium BC? List some similarities/differences.

C. THINK ABOUT IT

1. Suppose a friend asked you the intent and message of Song of Songs. How would you answer him or her?

2. Find two references from the Song of Songs where the message functions as an "antidote" for perversion and as a celebration of the propriety and dignity of human affection and sexual expression.

3. Can you find the themes of love and chastity in Song of Songs in other places in the Old and New Testaments? List a few locations.

D. READING CHALLENGE

Pick a chapter from Song of Songs to study and follow the steps below.

1. Read the chapter from the *dramatic* perspective.

2. Now read the chapter from the *typological* perspective. How has your interpretation of the poem changed after reading from these two different perspectives?

3. Pick two other perspectives from which to read your chapter and report how your interpretation differs or stays the same.

4. Give your preliminary opinion regarding the method of interpretation most suited to the Song of Songs. Support your answer.

26

FORMATION OF THE OLD TESTAMENT SCRIPTURES

NAME _____   DATE _____

A. OVERVIEW QUESTIONS

1. Over how long of a time period was the Old Testament composed? How many writers have been identified as authors of the Old Testament?

2. What are the five basic literary genres or types of the Old Testament?

3. In what languages was the Old Testament originally recorded?

4. Number the following writing systems in order from earliest in development to latest, and provide a brief definition of each.

    _____Syllabic writing system:

    _____Ideograms:

    _____Alphabetic writing system:

    _____Pictograms:

    _____Logograms:

5. Hebrew shares a common proto-Semitic alphabetic system with which other ancient dialects?

6. In light of ancient hand-copying practices, why was there an emphasis on "hearing" the word of the Lord in the Old Testament?

7. Who were the Masoretes? When did they live? What is the Masoretic Text?

8. When and by whom were chapter divisions added into the Old Testament?

9. What is textual criticism and what is its goal?

10. Define the following key terms.

   a. canon:

   b. messenger formula:

   c. Pseudepigrapha:

   d. Apocrypha:

   e. Tanak:

   f. Vulgate:

   g. Septuagint:

11. List the factors or criteria important to the selection process of the Old Testament canon.

12. How is it possible for the Hebrew canon to contain fifteen fewer books than the English canon but still also contain the same material?

13. Why was there confusion concerning the adoption of some apocryphal books into the canon?

B. THINK ABOUT IT

1. How do we know that the books included in the canon were inspired by God to be there? How would you answer a skeptical friend who asks you about your faith in the canon?

2. Which books are considered "disputed"? Does this affect your view of their status as canon? Why or why not?

Part V

THE PROPHETS

⚘ 27 ⚘

INTRODUCTION TO PROPHETIC LITERATURE

NAME ▨▨▨▨▨▨▨▨▨▨▨▨▨▨▨▨   DATE ▨▨▨▨▨▨▨▨▨

A. Overview Questions

1. What is a prophet? What are some of the titles for them in the Old Testament?

2. What is the difference between preclassical and classical prophets?

3. Moses was which type of prophet? (circle your answer)

   a. premonarchic

   b. preclassical

   c. classical

4. Jeremiah was which type of prophet? (circle your answer)

   a. premonarchic

   b. preclassical

   c. classical

5. Which two prophets were the earliest examples of classical prophecy within the Northern Kingdom?

6. Define the following key terms.

   a. eschatology:

   b. apocalyptic literature:

   c. fulfillment:

7. In what biblical books does the subgenre "apocalyptic" appear?

8. What is the difference between the *vision* and the *message* of a prophet?

9. Describe the difference between the prophet's message and the fulfillment of prophecy. (See Figure 27.2 on p. 508 for guidance.)

10. List the four major kinds of prophetic oracles and define them.

11. When a New Testament author says that a prophecy has been fulfilled, what is meant by that statement?

B. BACKGROUND STUDY

1. Where do we find prophetic texts in the ancient Near East? How were the classical prophets of Israel different from other prophets in the ancient Near East? What likely caused this change in Israel's prophetic movements?

C. THINK ABOUT IT

1. On page 513 the textbook states, "One must not become so absorbed in figuring out when and how fulfillment will take place that the message is neglected." What is meant by this statement? Do you agree? Why or why not?

D. READING CHALLENGE

Read the following passage combinations (and the context in which they appear). Discuss (1) the message of the Old Testament prophecy; (2) what is meant by the New Testament author regarding the prophecy; (3) and how the Old Testament prophecy should be read today.

a. Hosea 11:1; Matthew 2:15
b. Isaiah 61:1–2; Luke 4:17–21
c. Habakkuk 2:4; Romans 1:17; Galatians 3:11; Hebrews 10:38

RESEARCH PROJECT

Chapter 27

Pick a prophetic book and prepare a report with the following elements.

1. Research your prophet and report what you find concerning the time period in which he prophesied, the people to whom he prophesied, and his overarching message.
2. Pick a single oracle on which to focus. Place it within an oracle category (do so without consulting outside resources).
3. Describe the message of the oracle and comment on any prophetic fulfillment that may be related.
4. Give a theological application. What did you learn about God? How does this particular oracle affect your theology and/or your life?

❧ 28 ❧

ISAIAH

NAME ▓▓▓▓▓▓▓▓▓▓▓▓▓▓▓▓▓▓▓▓▓▓▓▓▓▓▓▓▓▓ DATE ▓▓▓▓▓▓▓▓▓▓▓▓▓

A. OVERVIEW QUESTIONS

1. What are the three key ideas found within the book of Isaiah?

2. Compare and contrast the actions of Ahaz and Hezekiah within the book of Isaiah. What do their actions reveal about Yahweh?

3. What is the main difference between the oracles of chapters 1–39 and those of 40–66?

4. Number the four historical scenarios in the book of Isaiah in the order in which they appear.

   _____Hezekiah's ill-fated alliances with Egypt and Sennacherib's siege
   _____The failure of Ahaz to trust Yahweh
   _____The transition from the Assyrian crisis to the Babylonian crisis and exile
   _____The return from exile

5. Is Isaiah considered a preclassical or classical prophet?

6. List the important parents of each of the following children, along with the meaning of the children's names.

   a. Immanuel:

   b. Shear-Jashub:

   c. Maher-Shalal-Hash-Baz:

7. What is meant by the term "kingdom eschatology" as it relates to the book of Isaiah?

B. BACKGROUND STUDY

1. Why has the unity of the book been the subject of so much controversy in biblical scholarship? Briefly outline the arguments for and against the book's unity.

2. List the two major events that serve as the focus of chapters 1–39.

3. Why would the Assyrian deportation program present a theological issue for the Israelites?

C. KEY PEOPLE

Add the following person to the chart in the back of the book (Appendix A) and then add his name to the prophetic timeline (Appendix B).

   a. Isaiah

D. THINK ABOUT IT

1. Pick one of the "Servant Songs" from Isaiah (42:1–9; 49:1–13; 50:4–11; and 52:13–53:12) to read. Write down any parallels you can see from New and Old Testament passages. Why do you think these songs have been included in Isaiah's message?

2. Why do you think the name "The Holy One of Israel" is so important in the book of Isaiah? Find a reference where this title is used. Do you think when and how Isaiah uses a name for God is significant?

E. READING CHALLENGE

Read Isaiah 1–6. What major themes of the whole book of Isaiah can you see in these six chapters? How would these chapters serve as a good introduction to the whole book? What can we learn about the purpose of the book of Isaiah from these chapters?

❧ 29 ❧

JEREMIAH

NAME ⬚⬚⬚⬚⬚⬚⬚⬚⬚⬚⬚⬚⬚⬚⬚⬚⬚⬚⬚⬚⬚⬚⬚⬚⬚⬚ DATE ⬚⬚⬚⬚⬚⬚⬚⬚⬚⬚⬚⬚⬚

A. OVERVIEW QUESTIONS

1. What about Jeremiah makes it seem as though we know him as an individual?

2. What part of the book of Jeremiah is similar to the scroll produced by Baruch?

3. Which sections of Jeremiah are thought to be later additions?

4. What is the purpose of the book of Jeremiah?

5. Where are the indictment oracles primarily found? What is the main indictment against Israel?

6. Where are the aftermath oracles primarily located? What is the message of these oracles?

7. What are the three major types of literary categories in Jeremiah?

8. Where are Jeremiah's "confessions" in the book? What is included in this category?

9. Describe God's policy with the nations as it appears in Jeremiah. Why is this significant for Jeremiah's audience?

10. Can we infer that the terms of the "new" covenant in Jeremiah are different from or the same as the Abrahamic covenant? Why?

B. BACKGROUND STUDY

1. Jeremiah's call came during the reign of which king of Judah?

2. Why was this time both a time of danger and a time of hope?

3. When was the final destruction of Jerusalem, and by which king?

C. KEY PEOPLE

Add the following people to the chart in the back of the book (Appendix A) and then add the prophet's name to the prophetic timeline (Appendix B).

   a. Jeremiah

   b. Baruch

D. THINK ABOUT IT

1. What are the implications of this statement: "There is nothing in Scripture to suggest that God has changed his policy for dealing with nations" (p. 539). What implications, if any, does this hold for modern-day political situations?

2. Read Jeremiah 31. In light of your answers to A.10 above, how should this passage be interpreted? Now read Hebrews 8. Are these passages related? In what way(s)?

E. Reading Challenge

Pick one of the following assignments.

1. Read Jeremiah 2–3. Based on your knowledge of Israelite history, determine what events you think Jeremiah is referring to. What purpose do these oracles serve within the context of the whole book? What do you learn about God's grace and judgment?

2. Read Jeremiah 19–20. What do you learn about Jeremiah from these passages? Reflect on the role and responsibilities of God's prophets. What role does suffering play in the call of God?

❧ 30 ❧

LAMENTATIONS

NAME   DATE

A. OVERVIEW QUESTIONS

1. In which division does Lamentations appear in the Hebrew canon?

2. On what Jewish feast day is Lamentations read annually?

3. According to tradition, who wrote the book of Lamentations? To whom do most biblical scholars assign its authorship?

4. Define the following key terms.

    a. catharsis:

    b. Zion:

    c. dirge:

5. What was to be the only consolation for "the Daughter of Zion" according to 4:21–22?

6. The poems of Lamentations were designed to do what for the survivors of Judah's fall?

7. What is the purpose of the alphabetic acrostics in Lamentations?

8. How many poems are in Lamentations?

9. What response did the removal of God's glory incite in the people? What *should* have been their response?

B. BACKGROUND STUDY

1. To what major event is the book a response? In what year did this event occur?

2. The "despairing" tone of the book indicates that the author likely did not know what? (circle your answer)

   a. the temple had been rebuilt

   b. Jeremiah had prophesied covenant restoration for Israel

   c. that Jehoiachin had been released from prison

   d. all of the above

C. THINK ABOUT IT

1. Review the eight categories of human suffering that were developed by R. B. Y. Scott. (See Figure 30.2 on p. 549.) Do you think these categories offer viable solutions to the problem of human suffering? Why or why not?

2. What does the book of Lamentations reveal about how we should respond to suffering in our own lives?

D. Reading Challenge

Pick one of the poems in Lamentations (they are divided by chapter) and address the following questions.

1. Is the poem you chose an acrostic?
2. In your own words, what is the main purpose and message of the poem?
3. Which of the key ideas (see p. 543) does the poet employ in your poem?
4. What modern-day theological application can be gleaned from the poem?

❧ 31 ❧

EZEKIEL

NAME ⬚⬚⬚⬚⬚⬚⬚⬚⬚⬚⬚⬚⬚⬚⬚⬚⬚⬚⬚⬚ DATE ⬚⬚⬚⬚⬚⬚⬚⬚

A. OVERVIEW QUESTIONS

1. Who was Ezekiel? From where did he prophesy?

2. Define the following key terms.

   a. Great Synagogue:

   b. "sons of the prophets":

   c. proto-apocalyptic:

3. List the three divisions of Ezekiel's message, including chapter references and a brief description of content.

4. What did the phrase "son of man" serve to emphasize in Ezekiel?

5. Why were the ecstatic visions of Ezekiel essential to the overall message of the book?

6. True/False: Ezekiel denied the teaching of corporate solidarity and instead preached only individual responsibility. (circle your answer)

B. Background Study

1. How can we determine the date of Ezekiel's writings?

2. List the kings of Judah in order from Josiah to Jehoiachin, noting how they lost their thrones. Also note when each Babylonian invasion occurred.

C. Key People

Add the following person to the chart in the back of the book (Appendix A) and then add his name to the prophetic timeline (Appendix B).

   a. Ezekiel

D. Think about It

1. Read Ezekiel 22. What do we learn about God and judgment from this passage? Why do you think this oracle was included? How would you describe the message of this chapter to a friend?

2. Read Ezekiel 33:21–33. In your own words explain Ezekiel's message. What do we learn about the people of Jerusalem at that time? What do we learn about God, his grace, and his judgment?

E. Reading Challenge

Pick one of the passages below and answer the following questions. (1) Which of Ezekiel's major themes or key ideas do you see present in these chapters? (2) Why do you think these oracles were recorded? (3) What can we learn about God and his presence from these chapters? (4) What modern-day applications can be gleaned from these oracles?

1. Ezekiel 1–3
2. Ezekiel 36–37

32

DANIEL

NAME ▮▮▮▮▮▮▮▮▮▮▮▮▮▮▮▮▮▮▮▮ DATE ▮▮▮▮▮▮▮▮▮▮

A. Overview Questions

1. In what century are the events of Daniel set?

2. Define the following key terms.

   a. pseudonymity:

   b. *vaticinium ex eventu*:

3. Why do some scholars date the authorship of Daniel to the second century BC? Why does the date of authorship *have* to be before 164 BC?

4. What are some reasons why Daniel might not be *vaticinium ex eventu*?

5. If the book was indeed written in the sixth century, who might have been the author?

6. When did the people of Israel expect the restoration of the Davidic kingdom? When did Daniel's visions reveal the restoration would take place?

7. What are the chapter divisions if Daniel is divided into halves? Why do some scholars think the book should be divided in this manner?

8. Briefly outline the parallel structure discussed in the book (see pp. 573–74).

9. Where does the term "son of man" appear in Daniel? Why is this title significant in the New Testament?

B. BACKGROUND STUDY

1. When did the final capital city of Assyria fall? What was the name of this city?

2. Why were the sons of Josiah constantly conspiring against the Babylonians? What did the Babylonians (especially Nebuchadrezzar) do about it?

3. What empire took over after the Babylonians?

4. Which Persian king was considered a deliverer? Why?

C. KEY PEOPLE

Add the following people to the chart in the back of the book (Appendix A) and then add Daniel's name to the prophetic timeline (Appendix B).

a. Daniel

b. Nebuchadrezzar

c. Belshazzar

d. Darius

e. Shadrach, Meshach, and Abednego

D. THINK ABOUT IT

1. What do you think Daniel's visions reveal about God's involvement in the rise and fall of empires?

2. Do you think the identification of the four kingdoms in Daniel is important? Why or why not?

3. Many people think the visions in Daniel are weird or hard to understand. Why do you think the visions were recorded in this manner? How would you explain their purpose to a friend unfamiliar with the Bible?

4. Is it a theological problem for the prophecies in Daniel to be recorded *vaticinium ex eventu*? Why or why not?

E. READING CHALLENGE

Pick one of the selections below and complete the following activities. (1) Compare and contrast the themes in your chapters. How are they similar? Different? (2) What do these chapters reveal about God and his interactions with his people in exile? (3) In your own words, what appears to be the main message of Daniel?

1. Daniel 1 and 6
2. Daniel 2 and 7
3. Daniel 3 and 8
4. Daniel 4 and 9

❧ 33 ❧

HOSEA

NAME ████████████████████████   DATE ██████████████

A. OVERVIEW QUESTIONS

1. During which century did Hosea live? To which kingdom did he prophesy and during which king's reign?

2. How are the Minor Prophets ordered in the canon (generally)? What is the name of this collection in the Hebrew Bible?

3. What are the "Judah" references? Why do scholars question their authenticity? Why might these references be authentic?

4. When did Hosea's mission to the Northern Kingdom likely end?

5. What did Hosea's relationship with his wife symbolize?

6. To what does the title "death-bed prophet of Israel" refer?

7. Define the following key terms.

    a. palistrophe:

    b. oracular prose:

8. What are the two main literary divisions of Hosea?

9. Number the following characteristics of preexilic writing prophets in the order in which they appear.

_____instruction

_____aftermath

_____judgment

_____indictment

10. Describe the double meaning of Israel's harlotry according to Hosea.

B. Background Study

1. Under which king did the Northern Kingdom experience her "golden age"? Why has this age been given this label?

2. Who was Hosea's earlier contemporary? How was his message received?

3. During the last thirty years of Israelite autonomy, how many kings were murdered?

4. What was the Syro-Ephraimite war? What was Israel's role in this conflict?

5. What jeopardized the monotheism of the Israelites?

C. Key People

Add the following people to the chart in the back of the book (Appendix A) and then add the prophet's name to the prophetic timeline (Appendix B).

a. Hosea

b. Gomer

D. THINK ABOUT IT

1. Review the views proposed regarding Hosea's marriage to Gomer. Which, in your opinion, is most likely? Why?

2. Why do you think the Israelites engaged in syncretism? What modern-day lessons can be learned from their mistakes?

3. What can we learn about God through Hosea's oracles and relationship with Gomer?

E. READING CHALLENGE

Read Hosea 1–3. In what ways does Hosea's relationship with Gomer parallel the oracle in chapter 2? Is the message of these three chapters primarily of doom or is hope included as well? How do you think an Israelite would have received Hosea's message?

❧ 34 ❧

JOEL

NAME _____   DATE _____

A. OVERVIEW QUESTIONS

1. What was Joel's vision about? To what did he correlate this vision?

2. What is meant by the term the "day of the LORD"?

3. Why is it noteworthy that Joel instructed the people to respond with the appropriate ritual?

4. What are the two oracles in Joel? What is the common denominator between the two oracles?

B. BACKGROUND STUDY

1. Why is the determination of the date of Joel important? Why is determining this date so difficult?

2. Which two centuries serve as the most likely candidates in which to date Joel's prophecies?

3. How is it clear that Joel was well versed in preexilic prophecy?

4. Why would a locust plague be so devastating to an ancient society?

C. KEY PEOPLE

Add the following person to the chart in the back of the book (Appendix A) and then add his name to the prophetic timeline (Appendix B).

a. Joel

D. THINK ABOUT IT

1. Where does Joel's prophecy appear in the New Testament? What do you think Peter meant by his use of this prophecy?

E. READING CHALLENGE

Read the book of Joel. What do you learn about God, especially concerning his judgment and mercy, from the book of Joel? Cite specific references to support your claims.

35

AMOS

NAME ████████████████████████████   DATE ████████████████

A. OVERVIEW QUESTIONS

1. Which minor prophets were contemporaries of Amos?

2. What was Amos's occupation, and what significance did it have for his message?

3. Number the messages of the prophet Amos in the order they appear in the book.

   _____Amos condemns specific acts of social injustice and religious hypocrisy.

   _____Amos relates five visions that deal with God's wrath and judgment on Israel.

   _____Amos denounces Israel's sin and forecasts national disaster.

   _____Amos reveals the promise of messianic restoration and blessing.

B. BACKGROUND STUDY

1. To what time period and during whose reigns has the book of Amos been traditionally assigned?

2. Where does Amos mention an earthquake? Has this event helped us to pinpoint the date of his prophecies?

C. KEY PEOPLE

Add the following person to the chart in the back of the book (Appendix A) and then add his name to the prophetic timeline (Appendix B).

   a. Amos

D. THINK ABOUT IT

1. Pick one of the five doctrines listed on pages 613–14. Read the Scripture references in Amos associated with it and reflect on what you find. Where else in the Old and New Testaments do you see teaching like this? How have you seen or not seen these principles applied in the church?

2. Read Amos 1:3–2:16. What are the sins for which the nations are convicted? How are the sins for which Israel is convicted the same or different? What does this comparison reveal about Israel and about God?

E. READING CHALLENGE

Read Amos 2:6–4:13. List all the verses where you see God is calling for social justice or action. What does this teach you about God's priorities and the actions he expects from his covenant people? What applications might there be for modern-day situations?

❧ 36 ❧

OBADIAH

NAME ⬚⬚⬚⬚⬚⬚⬚⬚⬚⬚⬚⬚⬚⬚⬚⬚⬚⬚⬚⬚⬚⬚⬚⬚⬚⬚⬚⬚⬚⬚⬚ DATE ⬚⬚⬚⬚⬚⬚⬚⬚⬚⬚⬚⬚

A. Overview Questions

1. What is the purpose of the book of Obadiah?

2. Who was Obadiah, according to later Jewish tradition? Who do modern scholars think he was?

3. Explain the significance of the word translated "vision."

4. Briefly outline Obadiah's three-part message.

5. What is *lex talionis*?

B. Background Study

1. What are the two most likely events about which Obadiah prophesies?

2. Who was the patriarch of Edom?

3. According to scholarly consensus, what happened to Edom?

C. Key People

Add the following person to the chart in the back of the book (Appendix A) and then add his name to the prophetic timeline (Appendix B).

    a. Obadiah

D. Think about It

1. What does Obadiah reveal about nationwide guilt? Do you think this principle still applies today? Why or why not?

2. What can be learned about God's interaction with pagan nations and with his people from this short book?

E. Reading Challenge

Read Obadiah and then address the following issues.

1. Discuss the significance of the genre and the format (see p. 623).

2. Pick one of the major themes of Obadiah (pride, *lex talionis*, universal judgment, or restoration). Where do you find this theme in the book?

3. Reflect on the theme you chose. Can you find this theme in the New Testament? If so, where?

4. In your own words, explain the message of Obadiah.

❦ 37 ❦

JONAH

NAME ▓▓▓▓▓▓▓▓▓▓▓▓▓▓▓▓▓▓▓▓▓▓▓▓▓▓▓ DATE ▓▓▓▓▓▓▓▓▓▓▓▓▓

A. OVERVIEW QUESTIONS

1. How is the book of Jonah unique among the prophetic books of the Old Testament?

2. Who is the author of Jonah?

3. What are some of the ways scholars have identified the nature of the book?

4. What are some objections that modern interpreters have to the historicity of the events in the book of Jonah? What are some of the reasons scholars give for its historicity?

5. Briefly explain what is meant by the equation Jonah = Nineveh.

6. True/False: The repentance of the Ninevites likely included a conversion to monotheism. (circle your answer)

7. What is the message of the book of Jonah?

8. What is the genre of the psalm in chapter 2? Why is this significant?

9. What is unique about the theodicy present in the book of Jonah?

B. BACKGROUND STUDY

1. In what century did Jonah live?

2. Who was the king of Israel at that time, and why was there great optimism in the Northern Kingdom during Jonah's lifetime?

3. Why have scholars been unable to determine the identity of the Assyrian king at the time of Jonah?

C. KEY PEOPLE

Add the following person to the chart in the back of the book (Appendix A) and then add his name to the prophetic timeline (Appendix B).

a. Jonah

D. THINK ABOUT IT

1. Why do you think Jonah was unwilling to preach God's message to Nineveh? What does the event with the fish reveal about the character of God?

2. What is a modern-day example to which a theological application from the book of Jonah can be made? Be specific.

E. READING CHALLENGE

Read the book of Jonah. Trace the themes of compassion, anger, and theodicy, listing references where these themes are present. Pick one of these three themes and reflect on what is revealed about it by Jonah's story. How does the story challenge any theological beliefs you currently hold?

❧ 38 ❧

MICAH

NAME ▓▓▓ DATE ▓▓▓▓▓▓▓▓▓▓▓▓▓

A. OVERVIEW QUESTIONS

1. In which other prophetic book is Micah mentioned? What is said about him, and what does this reveal about his career as a prophet?

2. Which sections of Micah do some scholars identify as later additions? What are some reasons why these sections might not be later additions?

3. What is the purpose of Micah's prophecies?

4. Briefly outline the five judgments predicted by Micah's five judgment oracles.

B. BACKGROUND STUDY

1. During whose reigns did Micah prophesy?

2. Which event of the great Assyrian crisis is generally thought to have served as the backdrop of Micah's prophecies?

3. What problems came with the economic growth of the early eighth century BC?

C. KEY PEOPLE

Add the following person to the chart in the back of the book (Appendix A) and then add his name to the prophetic timeline (Appendix B).

    a. Micah

D. THINK ABOUT IT

1. Read Micah 6:8. How does the context reveal that this verse might not be a statement about God's demands on humanity?

2. Read Micah 2:12–13 and 5:2–9. What do you think is the purpose behind these promises? Do you think these deliverers are to be identified with the Messiah? Why or why not?

E. READING CHALLENGE

Pick one chapter from Micah to study and answer the following.

1. Describe the purpose of that chapter in light of the message of the whole book.
2. Note any major themes present in that chapter.
3. Note what may be learned about God's requirements for his people.
4. Describe a possible theological application from this chapter.

❦ 39 ❦

NAHUM

NAME ▨▨▨▨▨▨▨▨▨▨▨▨▨▨▨▨▨▨▨▨▨▨▨   DATE ▨▨▨▨▨▨▨▨▨▨▨▨

A. OVERVIEW QUESTIONS

1. To what city does Nahum prophesy? What other Old Testament prophet prophesied to this city? How do the outcomes differ?

2. What is the most disputed section of the book? Why?

3. Why has it been suggested that Nahum owes a literary debt to Isaiah?

4. Who was the likely audience of this oracle? Why?

5. Why did the Lord tell of the fall of Nineveh beforehand?

B. BACKGROUND STUDY

1. When should the book of Nahum be dated?

2. When did the city of Thebes fall? What effect does this information have on the dating of Nahum?

3. Which two Judean kings are likely to be the subject of the favorable oracle?

4. What was the centerpiece of the Assyrian collapse?

5. What did Nineveh represent, despite its splendor?

C. KEY PEOPLE

Add the following person to the chart in the back of the book (Appendix A) and then add his name to the prophetic timeline (Appendix B).

  a. Nahum

D. THINK ABOUT IT

1. Though the judgment of God came upon the Assyrian Empire, and though Nineveh did indeed fall, the time until their judgment was long, and the people of Judah suffered under the yoke of Assyria. What does this example say about time and God's judgment? What does it say about God's grace for the oppressed and oppressor?

E. READING CHALLENGE

Read the book of Nahum. Compare and contrast the message of Jonah with the message of Nahum. What do these differences reveal about God's involvement in history? Are there any modern-day theological applications to be drawn from the message of Nahum? If so, what are they? Be specific.

❧ 40 ❧

HABAKKUK

NAME _____ DATE _____

A. Overview Questions

1. What distinguishes Habakkuk from the other prophetic books?

2. Which Old Testament prophet was likely a contemporary of Habakkuk?

3. What is the purpose of the book of Habakkuk?

4. What does the theophany of chapter 3 accomplish?

5. Where is God's twofold answer to Habakkuk's question? What is this answer?

6. Read Habakkuk 2:4. Where does this verse appear in the New Testament? What does it mean within the context of Habakkuk?

B. Background Study

1. When is it likely that Habakkuk prophesied? What internal evidence has assisted in this determination?

2. Match the description below with the correct person.

   _____Ashurbanipal
   _____Shamash-shum-ukin

_____Ashur-etil-ilani

_____Sin-shar-ishkun

_____Nabopolassar

_____Nebuchadrezzar

a. The son of Ashurbanipal who was handed the reigns of the Assyrian Empire.

b. The son of Ashurbanipal who seized the Assyrian kingdom from his brother after his father's death.

c. The Babylonian king who eventually sacked Jerusalem and began the Babylonian exile.

d. The brother of Ashurbanipal who, with the Elamites and Chaldeans, attempted to take control of Babylon.

e. The king of Assyria during whose reign the Assyrian Empire experienced extensive deterioration and division.

f. The first king of the Babylonian Empire who would bring the ancient Near East under Babylonian control.

C. Key People

Add the following person to the chart in the back of the book (Appendix A) and then add his name to the prophetic timeline (Appendix B).

a. Habakkuk

D. Think about It

1. Reflect on the following statement: "[God] began by suggesting that human responsibility lay not in having all the answers, but in responding to God in the proper way" (p. 664). Where does this principle appear in Habakkuk? Do you see it elsewhere in the Bible?

2. Reflect on the following statement: "Acceptance was not an act of philosophical nihilism . . . , but simply an act of trust" (p. 664). What does this statement mean? Has there been a situation in your life when you could relate to Habakkuk's question? How did you deal with your own uncertainty?

3. Pick one of the principles listed on pages 665–66. Describe where else you see that principle in the Old and New Testaments. Does God work this way in the lives of individual Christians? Why or why not?

E. READING CHALLENGE

Read the book of Habakkuk. Write down where you see each of the key ideas (see p. 659) presented. How should we relate the message of Habakkuk to current events?

❧ 41 ❧

ZEPHANIAH

NAME ▓▓▓▓▓▓▓▓▓▓▓▓▓▓▓▓▓▓▓▓▓▓▓   DATE ▓▓▓▓▓▓▓▓▓▓▓▓

A. OVERVIEW QUESTIONS

1. Which major prophet was a contemporary of Zephaniah?

2. What was the focus of Zephaniah's prophetic witness?

3. What was the purpose of Zephaniah's prophecies?

4. True/False: Zephaniah clearly predicted the siege and exile of Judah. (circle your answer)

5. What is the nature of the restoration projected in 3:9–20?

6. True/False: Zephaniah contains a series of oracles against the nations. (circle your answer)

7. To what does the expression "the day of the LORD" refer?

8. Which of the following qualify as the "day of the LORD"? (circle your answer)

    a. the end of time as we know it

    b. the overthrow of the Assyrian Empire

    c. the fall of Babylon

    d. none of the above

    e. all of the above

9. Define the phrase "world upside down." Where do you see it in Zephaniah's prophecies?

B. Background Study

1. What is a tentative date for Zephaniah's prophecies? What are the reasons why some scholars assign this date to his prophecies?

2. While Josiah's reforms may have succeeded in changing Israelite religious practices, what did they fail to do?

C. Key People

Add the following person to the chart in the back of the book (Appendix A) and then add his name to the prophetic timeline (Appendix B).

   a. Zephaniah

D. Think about It

1. The prophecies in Zephaniah indicate the judgment of God toward many nations, including Israel. Do you think God still judges nations in this way today? Why or why not?

2. Read Zephaniah 2:1–3. With your answer to the above question in mind, what do you think the role of the individual is in nationwide judgment? In other words, does nationwide judgment still affect the individual who serves God wholeheartedly? Why or why not?

E. READING CHALLENGE

Read Zephaniah 3. What is the nature of the judgment about to come on Judah? What is the nature of the restoration? Do you think that Zephaniah's prophecies refer to the end of time, to a historical situation that has already occurred, or to something else? Why or why not?

❧ 42 ❧

HAGGAI

NAME ⬚⬚⬚⬚⬚⬚⬚⬚⬚⬚⬚⬚⬚⬚⬚⬚⬚⬚⬚⬚⬚⬚ DATE ⬚⬚⬚⬚⬚⬚⬚⬚⬚

A. OVERVIEW QUESTIONS/BACKGROUND STUDY

1. What is the purpose of the book of Haggai?

2. Which prophet was a contemporary of Haggai?

3. To which period of Israelite history does Haggai's ministry belong?

4. What are the dates of Haggai's four messages (give the year, the name of the ruling king, and the month of each message)?

5. Who was Sheshbazzar?

6. Who were Zerubbabel and Joshua? How were they affected by Haggai's prophecies?

7. Number the following messages in the order in which they appear in the book of Haggai.

   _____God's intention to overthrow the nations and restore the fortunes of Israel
   _____A call to repentance and a challenge to rebuild the temple
   _____Zerubbabel will be "a signet ring" in Zion
   _____A rebuke to the community for their preoccupation with personal "comforts"

8. It is likely, in light of Ezekiel's vision, that Haggai saw the rebuilding of the temple as the cornerstone of what?

9. What did the temple symbolize to the postexilic community?

B. Key People

Add the following person to the chart in the back of the book (Appendix A) and then add his name to the prophetic timeline (Appendix B).

   a. Haggai

C. Think about It

1. Why do you think the evidence of literary skill in the composition of Haggai is important?

2. Try to put yourself in the shoes of a member of the postexilic community. Would Haggai's message be an effective motivator? Why or why not?

D. Reading Challenge

Read the whole book of Haggai. Write down references where you see the following:

   1. The use of varied phraseology:

   2. The use of chiasmus for emphasis:

3. The utilization of the rhetorical question:

What about Haggai's literary methodology is memorable or inspiring? Why do you think he spoke in this manner?

❧ 43 ❧

ZECHARIAH

NAME ▢▢▢▢▢▢▢▢▢▢▢▢▢▢ DATE ▢▢▢▢▢▢

A. OVERVIEW QUESTIONS

1. Who was a contemporary of Zechariah?

2. What was Zechariah's task?

3. What does Zechariah's name mean? Of what tribe was he likely a part? In what capacity did Zechariah serve in Jerusalem?

4. What is the traditional view of the literary integrity and dating of Zechariah? What are some ways in which some critical scholars disagree with the traditional view?

5. Zechariah's message included which of the following: (circle all that apply)

   a. encouragement

   b. warning

   c. rebuke

   d. exhortation

   e. indictment

6. What are the two main parts of Zechariah? Include chapter references and a brief description.

7. Define the following key terms.

   a. proto-apocalyptic:

   b. dispensationalism:

8. What is the significance of Joyce G. Baldwin's discovery of a chiasmic structure that underlies both parts of Zechariah?

B. BACKGROUND STUDY

1. Zechariah prophesied under which king of Persia?

2. How did the prophet Zechariah complement Haggai's message?

3. How long did Zechariah's ministry in Jerusalem likely last?

C. KEY PEOPLE

Add the following person to the chart in the back of the book (Appendix A) and then add his name to the prophetic timeline (Appendix B).

   a. Zechariah

D. THINK ABOUT IT

1. What does Zechariah's message and task reveal about God's desire for restoration?

2. How do you think the "eschatological day" of Zechariah relates to the eschatology present in the New Testament?

3. Where do you see social justice as a theme in Zechariah? What does this reveal about God's priorities?

E. READING CHALLENGE

Pick two chapters of Zechariah to read. For each chapter, answer the following questions.

1. Identify any messianic prophecies present. Where do they appear in the New Testament?
2. Identify any eschatological elements present. What do these elements reveal about the end-time teachings of the Old Testament?
3. Describe what you think the purposes of these two chapters are. How do they relate to the message of Zechariah's contemporary?

❧ 44 ❧

MALACHI

NAME ▓▓▓▓▓▓▓▓▓▓▓▓▓▓▓▓▓▓▓▓▓▓▓▓▓▓▓▓▓   DATE ▓▓▓▓▓▓▓▓▓▓▓

A. OVERVIEW QUESTIONS

1.   What does the name "Malachi" translate to?

2.   Why do some scholars think the book of Malachi was written by an anonymous author?

3.   What was the Great Synagogue?

4.   Define the following key terms.

   a.   iconography:

   b.   satrapy:

5.   List the six disputations of Malachi.

6.   What is the genre of Malachi?

7.   To what did Malachi's rhetorical-question-and-disputation format give rise?

8. Describe the role of Elijah in Malachi 4. How was this prophecy interpreted in the New Testament?

B. BACKGROUND STUDY

1. What does Malachi's position at the close of the English Bible Old Testament reveal about its chronological placement?

2. Why do some scholars consider Ezra and Nehemiah contemporaries of Malachi? When do they date the book's composition?

3. Of what is the expression "sun of righteousness" reminiscent and what does it reveal about Yahweh?

4. Why was the morale of the restoration community so low and apathetic?

C. KEY PEOPLE

Add the following person to the chart in the back of the book (Appendix A) and then add his name to the prophetic timeline (Appendix B).

a. Malachi

D. THINK ABOUT IT

1. What are the four elements of the disputational format? Locate an example of this format within the text of Malachi. What role do you think this format played in the delivery of Malachi's message?

2. Read Malachi 2. Why do you think Malachi focused so much on marriage and divorce in his prophecies? What, if anything, can we learn about God's view of marriage from Malachi's prophecies?

E. Reading Challenge

Read the book of Malachi and answer the following questions.

1. What parallels or common themes do you see with Haggai, Zechariah, and Ezra–Nehemiah? What differences do you see?
2. Summarize the theological message of Malachi. What does it say about God's priorities? What does it say about the responsibilities of God's people today?

❧ 45 ❧
WHAT WE HAVE LEARNED

NAME _____   DATE _____

A. THE ATTRIBUTES OF GOD

Pick one of the attributes of God highlighted in the textbook and answer the following questions.

1. Where in the Old Testament do you see this attribute highlighted? Be sure to expand your search of Scripture beyond the examples the textbook gives.

2. Give an example of this attribute from the New Testament.

3. Why is it important to know about this attribute of God?

4. How has this knowledge affected your reading of the Bible? How can you apply what you have learned to your everyday life?

B. False Dichotomies

1. Reflect on this statement: "The Old Testament God can be seen as a God of judgment and punishment, while in the New Testament he is personified as a God of love and salvation" (p. 722). Does this view come from an accurate reading of Scripture? Why or why not?

2. How would you respond to a friend that distinguishes between the "age of law" and the "age of grace"? What scriptural examples would you use to defend your position (either for or against)?

C. Central Theme

1. After reading about several different propositions regarding the central theme of the Old Testament, describe which theme sticks out to you the most. Why? How does this theme impact your reading of the Old Testament as a whole?

2. How would you summarize the plotline of the Old Testament?

≈ 46 ≈

RESPONDING TO GOD

NAME _____   DATE _____

A. OVERVIEW QUESTIONS

1. What did worship look like in the ancient Near East? How did it differ from worship prescribed by the law?

2. Reflect on the following statement: "Worship is a verb in the Old Testament" (p. 731). What does this mean? Explain.

3. Why was the knowledge of God essential to Israel's worship?

4. What are the words used in Hebrew to refer to worship? What do these words reveal about the nature of worship in general?

5. How did the Israelite sacrificial system differ from ancient Near Eastern sacrificial systems?

6. True/False: Israelite animal sacrifices were salvific in nature. (circle your answer)

7. Does the Bible's call to social justice idealize poverty? Why or why not?

8. What do the Old Testament laws aimed at providing justice for the socially disadvantaged reveal about the heart of God?

B. THINK ABOUT IT

1. Why are repentance and obedience considered prerequisites for worship in the Old Testament? Give scriptural examples.

2. Pick one of the spiritual characteristics below. (1) Define the characteristic you chose and (2) provide an example from the Old Testament where this characteristic is important.

   Devotion
   Thanksgiving
   Prayer
   Glorification

3. With what you know about the Israelite sacrificial system in mind, what significance is there to the term "Lamb of God" as it is applied to Jesus?

4. What are some practical applications of the Bible's call to social justice? Be as specific as you can and give examples other than those provided by the textbook.

❧ 47 ❧

THE JOURNEY TO JESUS

NAME _____   DATE _____

A. Overview Questions / Think about It

1. What is typology?

2. In what ways are the themes of the Old Testament continuous with the New Testament? In what ways are they different?

3. If a New Testament writer has interpreted an Old Testament passage outside of its original context, how do we account for the difference in interpretation?

B. The New Testament Use of the Old Testament

Pick one of the Old Testament references used at least eight times in the New Testament from figure 47.1 (p. 745). Look up each of its occurrences in the New Testament and note whether it pertains to God Almighty, Jesus as the Christ, or to humankind. Based on this analysis, what did the disciples of Jesus understand about these themes in the Old Testament?

C. Themes across the Testaments

Pick one of Martens's four basic purposes of Yahweh for Israel. (1) Define the purpose that you selected and (2) describe how it both captures the central message of the Old Testament and anticipates the person and work of the Messiah in the New.

1. Salvation/deliverance
2. Covenant community
3. Knowledge of God
4. Land of covenant promise

D. Conclusion

Briefly review the exercises in this workbook. How has this study of the Old Testament changed your theology over the course of the semester/class? What new things have you learned? What do you wish to study more in the future?

APPENDIX A

PEOPLE AND DATES

Name	Role (prophet, priest, king) and important relationship (country or family connection)	Period *abbreviations at foot of page; give century for kings and prophets*	Important Narrative Facts

P-Patr–Pre-patriarchal
Patr–Patriarchal

Ex–Exodus/Wilderness
Conq–Conquest

Judg–Judges
UM–United Monarchy

DM–Divided Monarchy
Exl–Exilic/Postexilic

Name	Role (prophet, priest, king) and important relationship (country or family connection)	Period *abbreviations at foot of page; give century for kings and prophets*	Important Narrative Facts

P-Patr–Pre-patriarchal
Patr–Patriarchal

Ex–Exodus/Wilderness
Conq–Conquest

Judg–Judges
UM–United Monarchy

DM–Divided Monarchy
ExI–Exilic/Postexilic

Name	Role (prophet, priest, king) and important relationship (country or family connection)	Period *abbreviations at foot of page; give century for kings and prophets*	Important Narrative Facts

P-Patr–Pre-patriarchal
Patr–Patriarchal

Ex–Exodus/Wilderness
Conq–Conquest

Judg–Judges
UM–United Monarchy

DM–Divided Monarchy
Exl–Exilic/Postexilic

Name	Role (prophet, priest, king) and important relationship (country or family connection)	Period abbreviations at foot of page; give century for kings and prophets	Important Narrative Facts

P-Patr–Pre-patriarchal
Patr–Patriarchal

Ex–Exodus/Wilderness
Conq–Conquest

Judg–Judges
UM–United Monarchy

DM–Divided Monarchy
ExI–Exilic/Postexilic

Name	Role (prophet, priest, king) and important relationship (country or family connection)	Period *abbreviations at foot of page; give century for kings and prophets*	Important Narrative Facts

P-Patr–Pre-patriarchal
Patr–Patriarchal

Ex–Exodus/Wilderness
Conq–Conquest

Judg–Judges
UM–United Monarchy

DM–Divided Monarchy
ExI–Exilic/Postexilic

APPENDIX B

CLASSICAL PROPHETIC TIMELINE

	To Israel	To Judah	To Foreign Nations
Assyrian Age			
Babylonian Age			
Persian Age			

A Survey of the Old Testament Video Lectures

A Complete Course for the Beginner

Andrew E. Hill and John H. Walton

Featuring 47 lessons on 4 DVDs, *A Survey of the Old Testament Video Lectures* features 11 hours of video content as it explores the literary, historical, and theological issues behind the Old Testament and its various books. A companion to the widely used textbook, *A Survey of the Old Testament*, these lectures are an ideal resource for students and independent learners who want an additional contact point with the material from the textbook to enhance their studies.

A Survey of the Old Testament Laminated Sheet

John H. Walton

This handy, at-a-glance study aid is ideal for last minute review, a quick overview of the textbook, or as an aid in Old Testament study. This resource contains six information-packed sheets that are laminated and three-hole-punched, making them both durable and portable. A companion to *A Survey of the Old Testament* by Andrew E. Hill and John H. Walton, this study sheet is an ideal resource for students and independent learners to enhance their studies.

Old Testament Today

A Journey from Ancient Context to Contemporary Relevance

John H. Walton and Andrew E. Hill

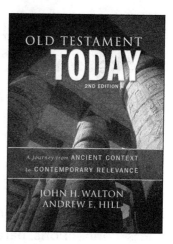

This proven Old Testament text with a wealth of full-color images helps readers connect the world of the Old Testament with today's world. *Old Testament Today, 2nd Edition*, is newly revised and includes a book-by-book survey, new maps and graphics, and other updates throughout.

Unique among Old Testament surveys, *Old Testament Today, 2nd Edition* not only provides an orientation to the world of the Old Testament, but also builds a bridge between the original audience and modern readers, demonstrating why the ancient message is important for faith and life today. It goes beyond basic content to help students understand what the Scriptures mean and how to apply them personally.

Taking readers progressively through the Old Testament, this text: (1) presents the details of the content, focusing on the story line, historical background, and literary information that address the original setting and audience; (2) focuses on theological perspectives and on issues of the author's purpose and the universal message of the text, building a bridge between the original audience and today's audience; and (3) develops an understanding of the relevance of the Old Testament writings to today's Christian, showing how they can be applied in personal faith and practice.

Available in stores and online!

Chronological and Background Charts of the Old Testament

John H. Walton

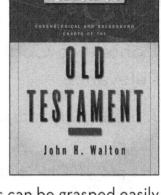

Charts provide visual organization that is ideal for teaching, learning, and review. Facts, connections, parallels, and contrasts can be grasped easily at a glance. This revised edition of Chronological and Background Charts of the Old Testament includes 42 new charts and 18 revised charts. The charts cover historical, literary, archaeological, and theological aspects of the Old Testament, its background, and biblical studies. Among the 100 charts are:

- Genealogies;
- Comparative Ancient Near Eastern Chronology;
- Parallels between Law and Wisdom;
- The Kings of Judah and Israel;
- Treaty Format and Biblical Covenants;
- Dynasties of the Northern Kingdom;
- Principles for Word Studies; and
- Messages of the Preexilic Minor Prophets.

Available in stores and online!

NIV Cultural Backgrounds Study Bible

Craig S. Keener and John H. Walton, General Editors

The *NIV Cultural Backgrounds Study Bible* is for readers who want to know more about what the stories and teachings of the Bible meant to its original authors and hearers.

The Bible was originally written to an ancient people removed from us by thousands of years and thousands of miles. The Scriptures include subtle culturally based nuances, undertones, and references to ancient events, literature, and customs that were intuitively understood by those who first heard the Scriptures read. For us to hear the Scriptures as they did, we need a window into their world.

The *NIV Cultural Backgrounds Study Bible* gives readers the insight they need to:

- Discover new dimensions to even the most familiar passages as they are taken behind the scenes into the ancient world.
- Find answers to puzzling passages by learning more about the context.
- Enjoy quick access to the most comprehensive collection of research about Bible times ever assembled in a study Bible.

Available in stores and online!

Genesis

John H. Walton

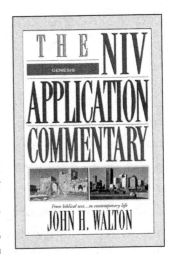

The Bible begins and ends with a revelation of God that gives redemption its basis. From the first verse of Genesis, the book of origins, we encounter a God of personality, character, purpose, and activity. Only in the light of what he shows us of himself as the creator of our world and the interactor with human history does the salvation story assume its proper context. Genesis sets things in order: God first, then us. Today, perhaps more than ever, we need God to put himself in front of us—to remind us who he is, and that he is. With characteristic creativity and uncommon depth, John H. Walton demonstrates the timeless relevance of Genesis. Revealing the links between Genesis and our own times, Dr. Walton shows how this mysterious, often baffling book filled with obscure peoples and practices reveals truth to guide our twenty-first-century lives.

Most Bible commentaries take us on a one-way trip from our world to the world of the Bible, but they leave us there, assuming that we can somehow make the return journey on our own. They focus on the original meaning of the passage but don't discuss its contemporary application. The information they offer is valuable—but the job is only half done!

The NIV Application Commentary Series helps bring both halves of the interpretive task together. This unique, award-winning series shows readers how to bring an ancient message into our postmodern context. It explains not only what the Bible meant but also how it speaks powerfully today.

1 and 2 Chronicles

Andrew E. Hill

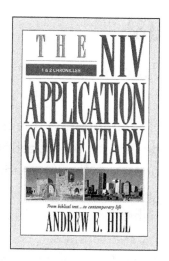

The Chronicles are more than a history of ancient Israel under the ascent and rule of the Davidic dynasty. They are a story whose grand theme is hope. Great battles are fought, heroes and tyrants vie for power, Israel splits into rival kingdoms, and the soul of God's holy nation oscillates between faithlessness and revival. Yet above this tossing sea of human events, God's covenant promises reign untroubled and supreme. First and Second Chronicles are a narrative steeped in the best and worst of the human heart—but they are also a revelation of Yahweh at work, forwarding his purposes in the midst of fallible people. God has a plan to which he is committed. Today, as then, God redirects our vision from our circumstances in this turbulent world to the surety of his kingdom, and to himself as our source of confidence and peace. Exploring the links between the Bible and our own times, Andrew E. Hill shares perspectives on 1 and 2 Chronicles that reveal ageless truths for our twenty-first-century lives.

Most Bible commentaries take us on a one-way trip from our world to the world of the Bible, but they leave us there, assuming that we can somehow make the return journey on our own. The information they offer is valuable—but the job is only half done!

The NIV Application Commentary Series helps bring both halves of the interpretive task together. This unique, award-winning series shows readers how to bring an ancient message into our postmodern context. It explains not only what the Bible meant but also how it speaks powerfully today.

Job

John H. Walton

Most people assume that the book of Job deals with the question of why righteous people suffer. Instead, John Walton suggests that the book is about the nature of righteousness, not the nature of suffering. As readers learn to deepen their questions, God will transform how they think about his work in the world and about their responses in times of suffering.

The majority of Bible commentaries take readers on a one-way trip to the world of the Bible, but they leave them there, assuming that they can somehow make the return journey on their own. They focus on the original meaning of the passage but don't discuss its contemporary application—the job is only half done!

The NIV Application Commentary Series helps bring both halves of the interpretive task together. This unique, award-winning series shows readers how to bring an ancient message into our postmodern context. It explains not only what the Bible meant but also how it speaks powerfully today.

Available in stores and online!

Zondervan Illustrated Bible Backgrounds Commentary Set

*John H. Walton,
General Editor*

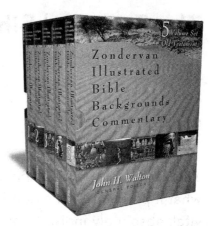

Many today find the Old Testament a closed book. The cultural issues seem insurmountable and we are easily baffled by that which seems obscure. Furthermore, without knowledge of the ancient culture we can easily impose our own culture on the text, potentially distorting it. This series invites you to enter the Old Testament with a company of guides, experts that will give new insights into these cherished writings. Features include:

- Over 2,000 photographs, drawings, maps, diagrams, and charts provide a visual feast that breathes fresh life into the text.
- Passage-by-passage commentary presents archaeological findings, historical explanations, geographic insights, notes on manners and customs, and more.
- Analysis into the literature of the ancient Near East will open your eyes to new depths of understanding both familiar and unfamiliar passages.
- Written by an international team of 30 specialists, all top scholars in background studies.

The Essential Bible Companion

John H. Walton, Mark L. Strauss, and Ted Cooper Jr.

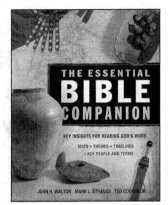

The Essential Bible Companion gives you what it promises, the essentials—the most vital, absolutely indispensable information you need for reading and truly understanding God's Word. Developed by two world-class Bible scholars and the creator of *The Bible in 90 Days* curriculum, this unique, easy-to-use reference guide gives you clear, crisp insights into the Bible book by book. From Genesis to Revelation, each book of the Bible has its key details laid out for you clearly and engagingly in a colorful two-page spread that includes:

- background information;
- timelines; and
- important biblical characters.

Striking a balance between too little and too much information—between the brief introductions provided in a Bible and the potentially overwhelming detail of a standard reference handbook—this well-designed, extremely helpful volume condenses the most important information in a highly visual, easy-to-understand format. Ideal for use as a companion to *The Bible in 90 Days* curriculum, *The Essential Bible Companion* is also a valuable resource for any Bible study. However you use it, this richly informative volume will assist you on your journey toward a well-grounded biblical faith.

Available in stores and online!